GOMPERS

Adam Rapp

BROADWAY PLAY PUBLISHING INC
New York
www.broadwayplaypublishing.com
info@broadwayplaypublishing.com

Cover photo by David Korins
First printing: February 2005
I S B N: 978-0-88145-259-4
Book design: Marie Donovan
Word processing: Microsoft Word
Typographic controls: Xerox Ventura Publisher 2.0 P E
Typeface: Palatino
Printed and bound in the U S A

GOMPERS was commissioned by City Theatre Company (Pittsburgh) and workshopped at their MOMENTUM 03: new plays at different stages, sponsored by Mellon Financial Corporation.

The world premiere of GOMPERS was presented by City Theatre Company (Tracy Brigden, Artistic Director; David Jobin, Managing Director) in May 2004. The cast and creative contributors were:

DENT	Danny Mastrogiorgio
NOLAN	Jeffrey Carpenter
SHOE	Kiff Vanden Heuvel
MOLLY	Molly Simpson
STROMILE	Demond Robertson
WHITE STEVE	John Magaro
POLICEMAN	Garbie Dukes
MRS GEORGE	Robin Walsh
CARLOS	Anthony Rapp
FINN	Bingo O'Malley
Director	Tracy Brigden
Set design	David Korins
Lighting design	Jeff Croiter
Costume design	Angela M Vesco
Sound design & original composition	J Hagenbuckle
Production stage manager	Patti Kelly
Dramaturg	Carlyn Ann Aquiline

CHARACTERS & SETTING

DENT, *the super. Apache's first lieutenant, early thirties, lives in apartment 2*

NOLAN, DENT'*s best friend, also works for Apache, thirty, troubled*

SHOE, *one of Apache's lackeys, under* DENT, *in love with* NOLAN, *late twenties*

FINN, *the old man in the courtyard apartment, seventies, a veteran*

MOLLY GEORGE, DENT'*s teenage girlfriend, sixteen, lives in apartment 4*

STROMILE, DENT'*s errand boy, black, sixteen*

WHITE STEVE, *another errand boy, white, thirteen, a thief*

POLICEMAN, *forties, hopeful, black*

CARLOS THE QUEER, *a gay man in his forties, white,* STROMILE'*s guardian, dying, lives in apartment 5*

MRS GEORGE, MOLLY'*s mother, forty, recovering addict, lives in apartment 4 with her daughter*

Setting: the waterfront, a train bridge, and various apartment units in a building on Jefferson Street

Time: the summer

Place: Gompers

ACT ONE

Scene One

(Apartment 2)

(Thursday. Late morning)

(The kitchen of a typical low rent bachelor pad. Cluttered and dirty. Newspapers and racing forms stacked about. A window facing the street. On the counter, a cheap radio. DENT is at the kitchen table, studying a dog racing program, listening to classic rock. He is early thirties, generally unkempt but has a well-groomed mustache. He wears a Van Halen concert T-shirt and faded cut-off jeans. He is barefoot. He sings along to 38 Special's Hold on Loosely *while reading the program.)*

(NOLAN enters wearing a white T-shirt under a blue bathrobe. He is late twenties, disheveled, unshaved. He is panting a little, uneasy. He clutches his stomach.)

(DENT stops singing, turns the radio off.)

DENT: Hey, Nolan.

NOLAN: Hey, Dent.

DENT: What's up?

NOLAN: Nothin.

DENT: You been out yet?

(NOLAN exhibits his take-out coffee.)

DENT: Fuckin river smells like shit today. I had to close the window earlier. I've spent all morning opening and closing it. You gotta wonder what they're dumpin in it... Is Shoe down there?

NOLAN: Yeah, he's there.

DENT: What's he doin?

NOLAN: Just sittin around. He said Apache's got somethin for us.

DENT: Did he say what?

NOLAN: Somethin in the building.

DENT: Great. Just when you think things are gonna slow down... I'm makin eggs, you want some?

NOLAN: No thanks.

DENT: I got rye toast, too.

NOLAN: I'm not hungry.

DENT: Nolan, you gotta eat more.

NOLAN: I eat.

DENT: No you don't. You drink coffee, you smoke those fucking menthols, and you top it all off with cheap bourbon.

NOLAN: So?

DENT: So you prolly have the insides of a catfish.

NOLAN: Nutrition's overrated. *(He removes a cigarette, lights it, smokes.)*

DENT: Gimme one of those.

(NOLAN gives DENT a cigarette, lights him. DENT smokes.)

DENT: Fucking menthols. It's like smokin a tube of toothpaste. *(He crosses to the stove, starts to fry some eggs.)*

DENT: You just woke up, huh?

NOLAN: Uh-huh.

DENT: Sleep any?

NOLAN: Not really.

DENT: Yeah, me neither. This heat. It's like thermonuclear and shit. Radio said it ain't lettin up anytime soon.... You hear Finn this morning? Seven-fuckin-thirty he's in the courtyard playin his trombone. Sounds like animal torture. I look out and the jackimo's dancing around in his bathing suit. A fuckin Speedo. Some legs on that guy. Talk about blind vanity.

NOLAN: Shoe says he was a major in the army.

DENT: No shit?

NOLAN: Fought in Korea.

DENT: That figures.

NOLAN: Apparently he's got all this stuff from the war in his apartment.

DENT: Like what?

NOLAN: Ribbons and Medals. His table cloth is an American flag.

DENT: Yeah, I'm sure he's a real patriot.

NOLAN: Shoe said he's got a saber mounted on his wall, too.

DENT: He prolly does, the wacko.... They got some hotshit new dog runnin tonight. Waterloo Rambler. Good weight. Flies outta the box. Can take a hit. Bobby Q swears by him. The tips are on their way right now.

NOLAN: Who's bringin em?

DENT: That nigger kid—Shlamiel, or whatever his name is.

NOLAN: Stromile.

DENT: Yeah, Stromile. I don't know about that guy.

NOLAN: Why?

DENT: He's a fucking junkie nigger.

NOLAN: He's not a junkie.

DENT: He's our most consistent customer.

NOLAN: Yeah, but he's not using.

DENT: How do you know?

NOLAN: I can just tell. Check out his arms next time. The kid's clean. He's prolly scorin for someone else.

DENT: He seems cagey to me. And what's with that name—Stromile?

NOLAN: I think it's cool.

DENT: You do?

NOLAN: Yeah, it's like "strong mile". Without the N and the G.

DENT: Typical nigger name.

NOLAN: When did you get so racist?

DENT: Since those motherfuckers from South Lock stole our V C Rs.

NOLAN: How do you know they were black?

DENT: Gut feeling.

NOLAN: ...I like Stromile.

DENT: You do?

NOLAN: Yeah. He has good energy.

DENT: Good energy? Whattaya work for the electric company?

NOLAN: I just mean he seems okay to me.

DENT: He lives with Carlos the Queer.

NOLAN: So?

DENT: So what the fuck is that about?

NOLAN: Carlos is his guardian.

DENT: Whatever. I hate fags. They should send em all to Mars or somethin. Now there's a space program...

(NOLAN *retches.*)

DENT: Bro, are you sick or somethin?

NOLAN: Sorta.

DENT: I mean, you look kinda funny.

NOLAN: Yeah.

DENT: You're like green.

(Suddenly, a GIRL's *voice from the street)*

GIRL: Hey, Ricky!

DENT: Shit.

NOLAN: Molly?

DENT: Yeah.

GIRL: Ricky Dent!

(DENT *goes to the window.*)

DENT: What?!

GIRL: I gotta talk to you.

DENT: Why?

GIRL: I just do. Tell Shoe to let me up. It's my building, too!

DENT: Molly, I'm busy.

GIRL: It's important.

MAN: Should I let her up?

DENT: *(Sotto voce)* Fuck.

GIRL: Let me up, Ricky! Come on!

MAN: Dent, she's been beggin for ten minutes.

DENT: *(Out the window)* Yeah, let her up, Shoe. But Mol,
first go over to the White Hen and get me a gallon of
milk. Two percent with the blue cap. Shoe, give her a
coupla bucks. *(He shuts the window, then opens it again.)*
My acid stomach's been acting up again. Girl's gonna
drive me to bestiality. I shoulda never fucked her.
*(He moves back to his eggs, stops the burner, salt and peppers
them, eats them in the pan.)*

NOLAN: Dent, I gotta show you somethin.

DENT: What.

NOLAN: Just this thing. Can I show you?

DENT: Sure.

(NOLAN opens his robe. DENT stops eating rather suddenly.)

DENT: Jesus, Nolan.

NOLAN: Weird, huh?

DENT: Holy fuck, bro.

NOLAN: Does it look bad?

DENT: Um. Yes, actually.

NOLAN: It's pretty intense, right?

DENT: That's a lotta blood.

NOLAN: Can you see my guts?

DENT: Um, I can see just about everything.

NOLAN: It's weird how we're put together, right?
Like our parts and stuff.

DENT: It's quite fascinating, yes.

NOLAN: Once you get past the muscle everything goes soft. We're like spaghetti and meatballs...

DENT: You need to go to a fuckin hospital, bro.

NOLAN: I do, huh?

DENT: I would. Jesus...

NOLAN: It looks that bad?

DENT: Yes, it looks that bad!

NOLAN: Do you think I'm dying?

DENT: I don't know, Nolan. What do you think?

NOLAN: I feel like I might be.

DENT: Maybe you should sit down.

NOLAN: Okay. *(He sits.)*

DENT: Did somebody stab you?

NOLAN: No.

DENT: Well, how'd that happen?

NOLAN: I did it.

DENT: Whattaya mean you did it?

NOLAN: I cut myself.

DENT: Was it an accident?

NOLAN: No, it was on purpose. I used a steak knife.

DENT: You cut your own stomach?

NOLAN: Uh-huh.

DENT: With a fucking steak knife?

NOLAN: Yeah, it was pretty sharp.

DENT: When did you do this, Nolan?

NOLAN: About an hour ago. I was in my kitchen lookin at all my silverware and this feeling just came over me so I started like attacking my stomach. It made me wanna cut my arm open, so I did that too, see? *(He pulls his sleeve up, revealing a gash.)* Weird, right?

DENT: That looks horrible, Nolan.

NOLAN: I used a paring knife on my arm. I was gonna do my other arm too but I got tired.

DENT: Wow, bro, you're really having a fucking crisis.

NOLAN: Yeah.

DENT: Well, what's wrong?

NOLAN: I don't know, Dent. I guess I'm just sorta lost or somethin.

DENT: Lost?

NOLAN: Yeah, lost.

DENT: Like confused?

NOLAN: I don't know. I guess.

DENT: Cause of the mill closing?

NOLAN: I don't think so.

DENT: About what then?

NOLAN: It's like everything I ever thought....

DENT: Everything you ever thought about what?

NOLAN: About myself... About this life... About... *(He doubles over in pain.)*

DENT: Take it easy, Nolan.

NOLAN: *(In pain)* It's all a lie, Dent! I've been livin a lie!

DENT: Don't strain yourself. *(Moving to help him)* We gotta get you to the hospital.

NOLAN: I don't wanna go to the hospital.

DENT: You need medical attention, bro.

NOLAN: No hospitals, Dent. Please.

DENT: Well, what are you gonna do?

NOLAN: I don't know. I was thinking about goin down to the river.

DENT: Why?

NOLAN: This black girl on the corner said that's where the Blue Jesus is.

DENT: What the fuck is the Blue Jesus?

NOLAN: The Jesus from that cross at Saint Jack's. A coupla months ago some kid from the high school painted it blue. That girl said it's walkin around on the water.

DENT: And you believe her.

NOLAN: I do, yes.

DENT: Since when did you get so religious?

NOLAN: I don't know. Jesus did some pretty cool stuff.

DENT: Nolan, did you hear what just came out of your mouth? You just said 'Jesus did some pretty cool stuff.'

NOLAN: He did.

DENT: He got fucking crucified, died, and was buried. That's noble, Nolan, not cool!

NOLAN: But he influenced a lotta people. He performed miracles and supported the golden rule.

DENT: He didn't support the golden, rule, he fucking created it!

NOLAN: Oh.

DENT: Nolan, let's concentrate on your stomach, okay?

NOLAN: Okay.

DENT: Did you clean it?

NOLAN: Um. Nuh-uh.

DENT: You should clean it, Nolan.

NOLAN: You think?

DENT: Yeah, bro. It could get infected.

NOLAN: With like soap and water?

DENT: Soap and water, shampoo, fucking kitchen cleanser, I don't care. You ever hearda gangrene?

NOLAN: Is that a band?

DENT: A band? It's a disease! It's when shit starts falling off.

NOLAN: Oh.

DENT: Yeah.

(NOLAN *doesn't move.*)

NOLAN: Hey Dent?

DENT: Uh-huh?

NOLAN: Before I clean it, can I look in the box?

DENT: Nolan, considering your present condition, I'd say lookin in the box might be a pretty low priority.

NOLAN: I'd really like to.

DENT: You need to get to the hospital, bro.

NOLAN: I'm the one who found it, Dent.

DENT: I know you found it, Nolan.

NOLAN: It was under that tree and me and Shoe found it! (*He doubles over in pain.*)

(*A knock on the door.*)

DENT: Fuck. (*To the door*)Hang on, Molly.

DENT *grabs a dish towel, hands it to* NOLAN. NOLAN *holds it to his stomach.* DENT *crosses to the door, opens it.* MOLLY *is standing there. She is 16, pretty, somehow lost, poor but hopeful. She wears track suit pants, running shoes, a T-shirt. She eases into the apartment, holding a gallon of milk.*

MOLLY: Hey.

DENT: Hey. *(He takes the milk, removes the cap, swigs.)*

MOLLY: Hey, Nolan.

NOLAN: Hey, Molly.

MOLLY: Sorry to interrupt.

DENT: Whattaya want, Mol? I got important business right now.

MOLLY: I gotta talk to you.

DENT: So talk.

MOLLY: In private.

NOLAN: You want me to leave?

DENT: No, you stay right there.

(DENT puts the milk in the refrigerator, takes MOLLY by the arm, leads her to the back of the apartment.)

MOLLY: Not so rough.

(While they are in the back, NOLAN dabs at his stomach with the towel.)

(SHOE enters. He is late twenties, pretty large, perhaps a little heavy. He wears a faded football jersey, long shorts, basketball shoes, a crewcut.)

SHOE: Hey, Nolan.

NOLAN: Hey, Shoe.

SHOE: What's up?

NOLAN: Nothin.

SHOE: You hear about the Blue Jesus?

NOLAN: Uh-huh.

SHOE: Pretty weird, right?

NOLAN: Yeah, it is pretty weird.

SHOE: This girl on the corner's been yakkin about it all morning. How it's bad luck if you see it.

NOLAN: It's bad luck?

SHOE: Yeah, so if you see it, don't bet on the dogs... You think it has anything to do with the thing in the box?

NOLAN: I don't know. Maybe.

(*Awkward pause*)

SHOE: So where were you last night?

NOLAN: I was around.

SHOE: I knocked on your door.

NOLAN: You did?

SHOE: Yeah, you didn't answer.

NOLAN: When?

SHOE: Ten-thirty, eleven. I knocked like twenty times.

NOLAN: I was out.

SHOE: Out where?

NOLAN: Just out.

SHOE: You were at the train bridge.

NOLAN: No I wasn't.

SHOE: Yes you were. You were sitting right in the middle of it. Your legs were hangin over the edge.

NOLAN: Were you following me?

SHOE: No.

NOLAN: You were. You were following me.

SHOE: I was just—

NOLAN: Don't fucking follow me, Shoe.

SHOE: Please don't do that.

NOLAN: Please don't do what?

SHOE: I don't like it when you call me Shoe.

NOLAN: Don't fucking follow me, Julius.

SHOE: ...Okay.

(*Pause*)

SHOE: Are you mad?

NOLAN: No.

SHOE: You hardly said a word to me.

NOLAN: When?

SHOE: Just downstairs.

NOLAN: I said hello.

SHOE: You practically grunted it. Did I do somethin wrong?

NOLAN: You didn't do anything wrong.

SHOE: Cause I thought we were sposed to get together last night. We had plans. We did have plans, did we not?

NOLAN: I need some space, okay?

SHOE: Why?

NOLAN: I just do.

SHOE: I don't understand.

NOLAN: Not now.

(*MOLLY enters from the back of the apartment crying. She exits. Moments later, DENT enters a little unnerved, perhaps slightly stunned.*)

SHOE: Hey, Dent.

DENT: Hey, Shoe.

SHOE: You okay?

DENT: Yeah, I'm fine. What are you doin up here?

SHOE: Oh, I, um, had to give you this. It's from Apache.

(He hands an envelope to DENT.*)*

DENT: Was he here?

SHOE: Yeah.

DENT: Did he seem pissed?

SHOE: A little.

DENT: Fuck.

*(*SHOE *hovers at the door.)*

DENT: Is there something else, Shoe, or are you not moving because you're having a stroke?

SHOE: What are you guys doin?

DENT: We're bakin fuckin Christmas cookies. What do you want, Shoe?

SHOE: I was wondering.

DENT: You were wondering what.

SHOE: If I could look in the box.

DENT: No.

SHOE: Why not?

DENT: Cause it's sleeping.

SHOE: I could watch it sleep.

DENT: I don't wanna wake it.

SHOE: Come on, Dent.

DENT: Come on what, Shoe? I'm the one who takes care of it.

SHOE: But me and Nolan found it and everyone knows that.

DENT: Whattaya mean, everyone knows that?

SHOE: I mean people know.

DENT: Like who?

SHOE: Like Dragan and Bobby Q.

DENT: Dragan and Bobby Q are everyone?

SHOE: No.

DENT: Who else?

SHOE: I think Kent knows, too. And Footy.

DENT: Great.

SHOE: It's no big deal.

DENT: It's a fuckin huge deal, Shoe! Did you tell Apache?

SHOE: Of course not.

DENT: You swear to god?

SHOE: I swear to god, Dent, I didn't say nothin. Nobody knows but those guys... Dent, I only got a few more minutes. Dragan's gotta go pick up those cell phones in Quincy. Please.

DENT: Jesus Christ, you guys are fuckin hooked. Hang on.

(DENT *exits.* SHOE *looks at* NOLAN. NOLAN *smokes.*)

SHOE: I wish you wouldn't smoke so much.

NOLAN: Why.

SHOE: Cause it makes me sad.

(NOLAN *smokes.*)

(DENT *returns with a cardboard box. He carries it very carefully. It is somewhat heavy. He sets the box on top of the table.* NOLAN, *and* SHOE *gather around it, peering down into the opening. Their faces go blank. Moments later they begin to laugh like children, mesmerized. After another moment,* SHOE *starts to reach into the box.* DENT *pushes him to the floor, seizes the box, exits to the back of the apartment.*)

(*The sound of a trombone coming from the courtyard.* DENT *returns.* SHOE *slowly gets up off the floor.*)

SHOE: I'm sorry, Dent.

DENT: Get out.

SHOE: I'm sorry, Nolan, I—

DENT: Shoe, go back downstairs and watch the fuckin door. Now.

(SHOE *exits.*)

DENT: Fuckin jackimo... That guy has absolutely no poise. I don't know how he was such a good football player... Jesus, my stomach. I gotta get some Tums or somethin.

NOLAN: What'd Molly want?

DENT: Nothin.

NOLAN: She was cryin when she left.

DENT: She's just stressed.

(NOLAN *doubles over again.* DENT *moves to the phone.*)

DENT: I'm callin you a fuckin ambulance, bro. (*He crosses to the phone, dials a number, waits. Into the phone*) Yeah, I need an ambulance.... Three-forty-seven East Jefferson... Yeah, down by the river... My friend got stabbed.... Three forty-seven... Okay. (*He hangs up.*)

DENT: They're on their way. Tell em you got jumped down by the river. Tell em it was those niggers from South Lock.

NOLAN: I don't have any insurance, Dent.

DENT: Didn't the mill take care of you?

NOLAN: Not really.

DENT: They gave you a severance package, right?

NOLAN: Yeah, but nobody got health insurance. You could get this thing called Cobra, but it's like three hundred a month.

(DENT *opens a drawer, lifts out a silverware tray, pulls out a knot of money, peels off several hundreds, hands them to* NOLAN.)

NOLAN: Thanks, Dent.

DENT: That's what friends are for, right? (*He opens the envelope that* SHOE *had given to him, removes a letter, reads, sighs.*)

NOLAN: What's it say?

DENT: We gotta do someone. Someone in the building.

NOLAN: Who?

DENT: Fucking Finn.

NOLAN: Why Finn?

DENT: I don't know. Poor sonuvabitch. My guess is Apache wants to jack up his rent. Finn's been in the courtyard apartment for like forty-some years. He pays like ninety bucks a month. With the new gambling boat coming and all that development going on down by the waterfront, Apache could easily get eight hundred for it, maybe even a grand.

NOLAN: You think?

DENT: He's charging Molly and her mom six. And Finn has a whole other bathroom. Rents are going up all over town, bro.

(The sound of a trombone from the courtyard.)

DENT: It's gonna be a long fuckin week.

(NOLAN smokes. DENT opens the refrigerator, takes another swig from the gallon of milk. Moments later, the sound of an approaching siren)

Scene Two

(The Riverfront)

(Noon)

(A park bench)

(STROMILE, sixteen, is sitting, waiting. He is black. He wears baggy shorts, a white T-shirt, patent-leather basketball shoes, a book bag.)

(The sound of a distant siren)

(MOLLY enters.)

MOLLY: What's up, Stromile?

STROMILE: Nothin.

MOLLY: Whatcha doin down here?

STROMILE: I ain't doin shit.

MOLLY: I'm not stupid.

STROMILE: Why a nigga always gotta be doin somethin?

(Pause)

MOLLY: How come you skipped the last week of school?

STROMILE: I had business to take care of.

MOLLY: What kinda business?

STROMILE: Nothin you need to know about.

MOLLY: You missed the carnival.

STROMILE: So.

MOLLY: They had a Cake Walk. Three-legged-races. Principal Larkin was in the dunking machine. Marky Bosano hit the bulls-eye three times in a row and Principal Larkin's toupee came off.

STROMILE: Good for Marky Bosano. I'm sure he'll go far in life.

(Pause)

MOLLY: You hear about the Blue Jesus?

STROMILE: No.

MOLLY: Tony Santaclause saw it walkin on the water yesterday. Right out there where they found the Crazy Carl's Catfish sign.

STROMILE: Who told you that?

MOLLY: Ebony Bunch. You know what the Blue Jesus is, right?

STROMILE: Yeah, I know what the Blue Jesus is.

MOLLY: Tony Santaclause told Ebony Bunch that his hair was blowin in the breeze and that his tongue was black. Pretty freaky, right? He saw it twice.

STROMILE: Tony Santaclause smokes that glass pipe.

MOLLY: I heard he quit.

STROMILE: He ain't quit shit. Fuckin crackhead.

MOLLY: Other people seen it, too.

STROMILE: Who?

MOLLY: Eljay Rice saw it on the train bridge. And that old lady who used to scream in the bowling alley saw him walkin on the train tracks.

STROMILE: The only place niggas be seein the Blue Jesus is up on the cross at Saint Jack's.

MOLLY: It disappeared two days ago.

STROMILE: That shit prolly melted in that hot ass church.

MOLLY: It's supposed to be bad luck if you see it. Ebony Bunch said the first time you see it you lose money. The second time you see it you die.

STROMILE: That's retarded.

MOLLY: After Eljay Rice saw it he lost fifty bucks at the dog track. The first time Tony Santaclause saw it he left his wallet on the bus to South Lock. After he saw it the second time he went swimming at the quarry and no one's seen him since.

(Pause)

MOLLY: *(Staring out at the river)* You notice how the water looks different?

STROMILE: No.

MOLLY: It's darker. The other day it looked purple.

STROMILE: So why you at the waterfront, then? Lookin for some bad luck?

MOLLY: I heard you were here.

STROMILE: See, you trippin again.

(Pause)

MOLLY: Guess what?

STROMILE: What.

MOLLY: I'm pregnant.

STROMILE: No you ain't.

MOLLY: Yes I am. Nine weeks. I ate a whole thing of black licorice this morning.

STROMILE: Maybe you just hungry.

MOLLY: Trust me, it's not hunger, Stromile. I've been pukin so much I gotta walk around with a plastic bag, see? *(Produces a plastic bag)*You should see all the stuff I've been eatin. Oreos. Vienna sausages. Sloppy Joes with peanut butter.

STROMILE: That's nasty.

MOLLY: *(Putting the bag away)* I quit smoking, too.

STROMILE: You ain't quit shit.

MOLLY: I did so. Threw my Merits in the river. Ask Ebony Bunch.

STROMILE: So who fucked you?

MOLLY: Ricky Dent.

STROMILE: Dent!

MOLLY: Uh-huh.

STROMILE: You let Dent fuck you? That nigga's like thirty-somethin years old.

MOLLY: So?

STROMILE: So he's got a mustache and shit. He could be your father.

MOLLY: I don't care. I like his mustache. And I didn't let him fuck me. He had to earn it.

STROMILE: Shit.

MOLLY: He did! He took me out!

STROMILE: Where?

MOLLY: Arthur Treacher's.

STROMILE: He prolly broke your skinny ass in half.

MOLLY: He didn't break nothin.

STROMILE: He bust your cherry?

MOLLY: No.

STROMILE: Tell the truth now.

MOLLY: I've been with other boys.

STROMILE: Who?

MOLLY: Boys at school.

STROMILE: Stop lyin, Molly.

MOLLY: I have. I was with Brad Lee.

STROMILE: *Brad Lee* fucked you?

MOLLY: Yep.

STROMILE: When?

MOLLY: When we went to that museum in Quincy.
He did me in the mummy room. And I was with
Dougie Dyd, too.

STROMILE: For real?

MOLLY: Right over there on that other picnic table. He
carved the date in the wood. That boy was good, too.

STROMILE: I heard Douggie Dyd's got three nuts.

MOLLY: Well he doesn't.

STROMILE: Eenie, Meenie, and Mynie.

MOLLY: You're just jealous.

STROMILE: Shit. *(Pause)* Damn, Molly.

MOLLY: What.

STROMILE: You like a hoe and shit.

MOLLY: I'm not a hoe!

STROMILE: Well not no more. Not if Dent's fuckin you.
If Dent's fuckin you, you property now. You like a car
and shit. You like his Audie.

MOLLY: I'm not a car, Stromile! And Ricky Dent's not just fuckin me, he's with me.

STROMILE: Shit.

MOLLY: He is.

STROMILE: It ain't like you goin together.

MOLLY: He loves me and I love him and that's all that matters.

STROMILE: You gonna have the baby?

MOLLY: Yep.

STROMILE: I wouldn't.

MOLLY: Why not?

STROMILE: Cause that nigga ain't gonna marry you.

MOLLY: He might.

STROMILE: What if he don't? Who gonna help you?

MOLLY: My ma.

STROMILE: Uh-huh.

MOLLY: She is, Stromile.

STROMILE: She can't even help herself.

MOLLY: She's doin a lot better lately. She started goin to this alcoholics group in South Lock. She's got a sponsor and everything... (Touching her stomach) I hope it's a girl. If it's a girl I'm gonna name it Magdalena. You like that name?

STROMILE: Not really.

MOLLY: Why not?

STROMILE: That's like Puerto Rican.

MOLLY: So.

STROMILE: So you ain't Puerto Rican, Molly, you white. And Dent's white, too.

MOLLY: I can name my baby whatever I want... Wanna feel it?

STROMILE: Feel what?

MOLLY: My belly.

STROMILE: You trippin.

MOLLY: It's all warm and hard.

STROMILE: Keep that shit to yourself.

MOLLY: *(Pulling her shirt up)* Come on, Stromile. You got those nice soft hands.

(He hesitates, then places his hand on her stomach.)

MOLLY: You can press harder than that.

(He presses harder.)

MOLLY: I imagine her doin stuff, Stromile. Like bein in a crib. Playin with blocks. Takin milk from me. Can you feel her? My little Magdalena?

(STROMILE puts his other hand on her stomach. They stare at each other for a long moment.)

(WHITE STEVE enters. He is thirteen, white, tiny, crazy. He wears basketball shoes that are too big, baggy pants, a hockey jersey, and a baseball hat cocked funny on his head. He carries a saber at his side. He is also holding an enormous ice cream cone. He licks it throughout.)

(STROMILE takes his hand away.)

WHITE STEVE: Whatchu doin?

STROMILE: Nothin.

WHITE STEVE: Yes you are.

STROMILE: Mind your business, Steve.

WHITE STEVE: I'm tellin Dent.

STROMILE: You tell Dent I'll bust your ass.

WHITE STEVE: You gotta catch me first.

STROMILE: Oh, believe me I'll catch you. Little herky-jerky bitch.

(WHITE STEVE *laughs, fidgets.*)

WHITE STEVE: Hey, Molly.

MOLLY: Hey, Steve.

WHITE STEVE: Wanna lick?

MOLLY: No.

WHITE STEVE: There ain't much left. It's Napoleon.

STROMILE: Neapolitan!

WHITE STEVE: Yeah, that.

STROMILE: Knucklehead.

(WHITE STEVE *takes a few more licks and then throws his ice cream cone into the river.*)

WHITE STEVE: *(To* MOLLY*)* Got a square?

MOLLY: No.

WHITE STEVE: Yes you do. You got them Merits.

MOLLY: No I don't, I quit.

WHITE STEVE: Booshit.

MOLLY: Didn't I, Stromile?

STROMILE: She say she quit she quit.

WHITE STEVE: Snap. *(He fidgets a bit, takes half a cigarette out of his pocket, lights it, smokes for a moment, flicks the butt out in the darkness.)* You like my cutlass?

MOLLY: Your what?

WHITE STEVE: My cutlass. Pretty crisp, ain't it? *(He takes out his sword, flails it about, kills an invisible foe, puts it back in his scabbard.)*

STROMILE: Where'd you get that?

WHITE STEVE: I found it.

STROMILE: Stop lyin.

WHITE STEVE: I ain't lyin.

STROMILE: You stole that shit.

WHITE STEVE: I found it in the parking lot at the dog track.

STROMILE: Foolish-ass nigga.

(WHITE STEVE pushes the scabbard toward MOLLY.)

WHITE STEVE: You wanna touch it, right?

MOLLY: Keep that thing away from me.

(WHITE STEVE pokes her with it.)

WHITE STEVE: I'll let you touch it for a dollar.

MOLLY: Stop, Steve!

WHITE STEVE: I saw Stromile feelin on you.

STROMILE: You didn't see shit.

WHITE STEVE: Molly George, George Molly.

MOLLY: Steve White, White Steve.

WHITE STEVE: When you gonna let me feel you like that, Molly?

MOLLY: Maybe when you grow a little.

WHITE STEVE: Shit, I'm big, you just don't know where.

MOLLY: The space between your ears, maybe.

WHITE STEVE: Space between your titties.

(MOLLY gives WHITE STEVE the finger.)

STROMILE: Yo, Steve, you got the digits or what?

WHITE STEVE: I got em.

STROMILE: Well let me get them joints so I can get the fuck up outta here.

(WHITE STEVE *reaches behind him, removes a racing form, hands it to him.* STROMILE *starts to look through it.*)

STROMILE: Who gave you these?

WHITE STEVE: Coca Cola Joe.

STROMILE: They circled.

WHITE STEVE: So?

STROMILE: Knucklehead.

WHITE STEVE: What?

STROMILE: You know Dent wants them joints highlighted.

WHITE STEVE: Coca Cola Joe didn't have no highlighter.

STROMILE: What about the one Nolan gave you to give to him?

WHITE STEVE: I gave it to him!

(STROMILE *puts it in his book bag.*)

STROMILE: What about that other thing?

WHITE STEVE: I got it.

STROMILE: Well give it up.

WHITE STEVE: Where's my flow?

(STROMILE *reaches into his pocket, removes an envelope, hands it to* WHITE STEVE. *He opens it, takes out two fives.*)

WHITE STEVE: Ten bones! They said twinny!

STROMILE: Well, that's what you got.

WHITE STEVE: Cheap bitches! *(He stuffs the money into his pocket.)*

STROMILE: I don't got time to be playin, Steve.

(WHITE STEVE removes a small vial from his pocket, holds it out in front of STROMILE. STROMILE snatches it from him.)

WHITE STEVE: What is it?

STROMILE: It ain't none of your motherfuckin business is what it is.

WHITE STEVE: It's poison, ain't it.

STROMILE: Stoopid.

WHITE STEVE: I heard Bobby Q talkin about it at the track. It's a special kinda poison cause it don't have no taste and it won't show up in no hospital report. Apache's gonna do someone.

STROMILE: Apache ain't gonna do nobody. And it ain't poison. Doofy-ass knucklehead.

WHITE STEVE: Take some then.

(STROMILE shakes his head, aggravated.)

WHITE STEVE: See? I'm right, ain't it?

(STROMILE puts the vial in his book bag, zippers it, sling it over his shoulder.)

WHITE STEVE: Guess what I got?

STROMILE: What, herpes?

WHITE STEVE: No. Check it out? *(He pulls out a small plastic baggie containing a hypodermic needle.)*

MOLLY: What is that?

WHITE STEVE: It's a AIDS needle.

STROMILE: Stop lyin.

WHITE STEVE: It is.

STROMILE: Where'd you get it?

WHITE STEVE: From that junkie's garbage.

STROMILE: What junkie's garbage?

WHITE STEVE: Carlos the Queer.

STROMILE: Why you pickin through niggas' garbage?

WHITE STEVE: You can find good shit in the garbage.

MOLLY: What are you gonna do with that?

WHITE STEVE: I don't know. I might stick somebody if they get too close.

STROMILE: You'll prolly stick your damn self. Foolish ass.

(Suddenly, a POLICEMAN *appears. He is black, fortyish.* WHITE STEVE *hides the plastic baggie.)*

POLICEMAN: How you kids doin?

(No one answers.)

POLICEMAN: Silence is bliss, huh? *(To* STROMILE*)* Everything okay, partner?

STROMILE: I'm straight.

POLICEMAN: You straight?

STROMILE: Uh-huh.

POLICEMAN: Lines are straight. Lines and pencils. You a line?

STROMILE: No.

POLICEMAN: You a pencil?

STROMILE: I ain't nothin. I'm just chillin.

POLICEMAN: You chillin?

WHITE STEVE: Yeah, we chillin.

POLICEMAN: Oh, you chillin, too?

WHITE STEVE: Chillin like Bob Dylan.

POLICEMAN: Bob Dylan, huh?

WHITE STEVE: Yup.

POLICEMAN: Do you even know who Bob Dylan is?

WHITE STEVE: I know who he is.

POLICEMAN: Who?

WHITE STEVE: A man.

POLICEMAN: What's your name, son?

WHITE STEVE: Why?

POLICEMAN: Cause I asked you, that's why.

WHITE STEVE: I don't gotta tell you.

POLICEMAN: You don't, do you?

WHITE STEVE: Nope.

MOLLY: His name is Steve.

WHITE STEVE: Shut up, Molly!

MOLLY: Steve White. But everybody calls him White Steve.

WHITE STEVE: Everybody calls you trick-ass-bitch!

(She gives him the finger.)

POLICEMAN: Steve, huh? Yeah, you look like a Steve.

WHITE STEVE: You look like a kangaroo.

POLICEMAN: I do?

WHITE STEVE: Yup. So why don't you just hop on outta here and leave us alone.

POLICEMAN: You don't watch it I'll hop your ass over to the juvy hall is where I'll hop. Hamstock ain't but a few miles down the road.

WHITE STEVE: Shoo.

POLICEMAN: Where you live, little man?

WHITE STEVE: On the earth.

POLICEMAN: Is that right?

WHITE STEVE: Did I stutter?

POLICEMAN: You a earthling?

WHITE STEVE: I ain't no Martian.

POLICEMAN: Your parents know you down here?

MOLLY: White Steve don't have no parents.

WHITE STEVE: Yes I do!

MOLLY: No he don't. He don't have no parents and he still sucks his thumb.

WHITE STEVE: Well, your mama smells like vinegar cause she's gotta douche so much.

MOLLY: You don't even know what a douche is.

WHITE STEVE: Yes I do.

MOLLY: What is it?

WHITE STEVE: It's when skanky bitches clean their pussies with salad dressing.

STROMILE: So stoopid!

POLICEMAN: What's that you carryin, Steve?

WHITE STEVE: What, this?

POLICEMAN: Yeah, that.

WHITE STEVE: It's my cutlass.

POLICEMAN: Your cutlass, huh?

WHITE STEVE: Yep. Pretty crisp, ain't it?

POLICEMAN: Where'd you get it?

WHITE STEVE: I found it.

POLICEMAN: You found it.

WHITE STEVE: Uh-huh.

POLICEMAN: *(To* MOLLY*)* That's an awfully unusual thing to find, don't you think, Molly?

MOLLY: Maybe.

POLICEMAN: What about you, youngblood?

STROMILE: What about me?

POLICEMAN: Steve's cutlass. Awfully unusual thing to find, right?

STROMILE: I find shit all the time.

POLICEMAN: I'm sure you do, little brother, I'm sure you do.... Steve, if you don't mind me askin, what are you plannin on doin with that?

WHITE STEVE: Why, you wanna buy it? I'll sell it to you for a hundred.

POLICEMAN: You a business man, huh?

WHITE STEVE: Yup.

POLICEMAN: Clockin gees, makin bank?

WHITE STEVE: You know it.

POLICEMAN: Just do me a favor and keep that thing put away, okay, Scarface? You don't wanna hurt nobody, now, do you?

WHITE STEVE: I ain't gonna hurt nobody.

POLICEMAN: Okay then, that's good to know *(To* STROMILE*)* What about you, son, what's your name?

STROMILE: I ain't your son.

POLICEMAN: No you ain't either. What's your name?

STROMILE: Ronald.

POLICEMAN: Ronald what?

STROMILE: McDonald.

POLICEMAN: You think you're pretty smart, huh?

STROMILE: No.

POLICEMAN: All you kids these days. Smokin reefer.
Drinkin forties. Droppin outta high school like it's some
kinda bus you think you can just stop ridin. Makes no
damn sense to me.
   I'll tell you what, things are changin around here.
We got that gamblin boat comin. Coupla strip malls.
Three-story parkin garage. Lotsa prime development.
This whole area's gettin built up. They plantin ficus
trees all up and down the waterfront. Improvements...
You kids stay outta trouble, now, you hear?

STROMILE: We ain't in no trouble.

POLICEMAN: Well you just be sure to keep it that way.
They're shooting off the fireworks this weekend so
there's gonna be all types of stuff goin on down here.

(The POLICEMAN *exits, whistling.* WHITE STEVE *gives him
the finger, undetected.)*

WHITE STEVE: Trick-ass pig.

STROMILE: You better get back to the track,
knucklehead. Bobby Q might have some greyhound
shit for you to shovel.

WHITE STEVE: I'm goin.

STROMILE: You lucky you got that job. Just cause you
white.

WHITE STEVE: I can't help it if Bobby Q don't like
niggers.

*(*STROMILE *starts after* WHITE STEVE. WHITE STEVE *pulls
out his needle.* STROMILE *stops.)*

STROMILE: Yeah, go head and stick me. I'll drown your
sorry ass right in that river... Go on.

(WHITE STEVE *turns, runs away laughing.*)

STROMILE: Little punk.

MOLLY: He's just scared, that's why he acts like that.

(Pause)

STROMILE: Lemme get up outta here. River fuckin stinks today. *(He starts to leave.)*

MOLLY: Stromile!

STROMILE: *(Stopping)* What.

MOLLY: You goin to the fireworks this weekend?

STROMILE: I don't know. Maybe.

MOLLY: Wanna go with me?

STROMILE: What about Dent?

MOLLY: He's got stuff to do... I was gonna climb the train bridge.

STROMILE: You can't climb no train bridge.

MOLLY: Yes I can.

STROMILE: You pregnant, Molly.

MOLLY: The doctor said it's important to stay active. I walk two miles every morning. Will you come?

STROMILE: What time?

MOLLY: Like nine o'clock.

STROMILE: Fuck it, I'll be there. But don't tell nobody.

MOLLY: I won't.

STROMILE: Especially that little fool.

MOLLY: It's just between you and me.

STROMILE: *(Exiting)* Aaight, I'll see you. I gotta go.

MOLLY: Stromile.

(He stops, turns.)

MOLLY: You wanna touch it again?

(She lifts her shirt. STROMILE *hesitates, then touches her belly, somehow magnetized. Some voices off in the distance.* STROMILE *retracts his hand, runs into the darkness.)*

*(*MOLLY *sits on the picnic table, draws her knees into her chest, stares out at the water. After a moment she turns around, facing away from the water. She pulls her plastic bag out, vomits.)*

Scene Three

(Thursday. Early evening)

(Apartment #4)

(The living room. Cheap furniture. Magazines cluttered. A T V is on a game show, the sound turned low. Baskets of unfolded laundry. A failed attempt at domestic upkeep.)

*(*MOLLY's *mother,* MRS GEORGE, *is sitting on the sofa, playing solitaire, talking on a cordless phone. She is early forties.)*

MRS GEORGE: Yeah, they're takin applications as early as next week. I think I can do it, Reenie. My hands are really gettin used to the cards. I cut myself the other day, though... Oh, it's no big deal, it's just a paper cut. Ramona said they won't hire you if you got ugly hands... *(Looking at her nails)* Yeah, I'm gonna get em done. I'll prolly try that new place over by where the mill used to be. Century Nails or whatever it's called... Oh, I can get there. I'll just take the bus or somethin... Reenie, I don't mind the bus, it's safe enough...

No, I haven't seen Molly today.... Yeah, nine weeks along. I can't believe it... No, she's not really showin yet. She's so tiny you know? When I was carryin Jimmy some people didn't even know I was pregnant eight months into it... Yeah, she says she's gonna have it.... Our super, of all people. Richard Dent... He's in his thirties. He's cute, too, Reenie. He's got this mustache.... I think he's involved with some kinda private business, too. Wholesale items or somethin. You can't knock an entrepreneur.

Yeah, me and Mol been gettin along pretty good lately. She forgave me for that whole thing with her softball coach... Yeah, he still calls once in a while but I keep him at a distance. She's had a lotta patience with me, Reenie. I don't know where that girl gets her grace from. Certainly not from her father... No, I haven't heard from him. I think he's down in Texas. He's prolly knockin off A T Ms or somethin intelligent like that... We're gonna turn Jimmy's old room into the baby's room... Yeah, new wallpaper and everything... Oh, he's still overseas... He was in Bagdad last time he called.... A few weeks ago. He sends me money and stuff, he's such a good guy... Yeah, I love him so much. I told him I was sober and he was real proud...

(The sound of a distant trombone.)

MRS GEORGE: Oh, Reenie, can you hear that?... It's a trombone... Yeah, a real trombone... This old man's been playing it in the courtyard. I think he's crazy or somethin... It sounds so sad, I can hardly stand it... Hang on I'm gonna close the window.

(MRS GEORGE rises, closes the living room window. The sound of the trombone is muffled now.)

MRS GEORGE: Hey... Yeah, where were we?... You know, Reenie, it hasn't been that bad.... I got real tempted the other day but I just breathed through it and did some of the prayers and then you called and it passed....

Hey, guess what?... I'm thinkin about startin yoga.... Yeah, there's a guy in group who swears by it. He's

always carryin this little blue mat around. He unrolled
it and let me kneel on it. Those things are pretty
comfortable.... No, I think he's gay. Yeah, he's too
tan to be straight.... Brian Von Drake or Von Drasek
or something.
Yoga's sposed to be so good for you, Reenie. It's all
about breathin and concentration and overcoming pain
and stuff.... Yeah, physically and spiritually... Well,
Brian goes to this place by the dog track.... I know,
isn't that funny? Gambling and yoga...

*(She stops dealing cards, rises, opens one of the doors to the
T V stand, pulls out a bottle of vodka, sets it on the coffee
table in front of her.)*

MRS GEORGE: Okay, Reenie... Well, thanks for talkin,
I appreciate you takin the time. Sometimes it's just
good to hear a friendly voice... No, I'm doin real good,
I promise... Okay ...Okay, bye, Reenie.

*(MRS GEORGE hangs up. She stares at the bottle of vodka.
She touches it, starts to unscrew it, stops, rises, walks away
from it, cries. After a moment, she seizes the bottle, turns,
places it back inside the T V stand, turns back to the coffee
table, deals herself a game of solitaire.)*

Scene Four

(Thursday. Early evening)

(Apartment #2)

(DENT is on the phone.)

DENT: *(Into phone)* Yeah, you said they were gonna be at
the loading dock.... The fucking loading dock over by
the old Goldblatts... Yeah, in Quincy... Well supposedly
four hundred units... Those ones with the cameras in
em... I don't know what to do, Stavros. Maybe you

should tell me.... I got three of my guys down there scratchin their fucking balls.

(A knock at the door)

DENT: *(Into phone)* Hang on...

(DENT crosses to the front door with the phone, opens the door. SHOE enters.)

SHOE: The kid wants to cop.

DENT: Send him in.

SHOE: Send him in? Since when did you start letting people in here?

DENT: Shoe, send the fucking kid in here and go back downstairs.

(SHOE exits. STROMILE enters. DENT motions for him to enter, closes the door, exits to the back, continuing to talk on the phone. STROMILE stands near the door, reaches into his pocket, removes fifty dollars, waits.)

DENT: *(Offstage, talking in phone)* Well, if you're gonna continue to conduct your business like a jackimo I'll make arrangements with someone else. I know Stu Ship in Flossmore is achin to get connected... And that guy shows up when he says he's gonna show up... *(He re-enters holding a small packet of paper containing heroin. Into phone)* Well, then get your shit together, Stavros. Save your apologies for someone else.

(DENT hangs up, offers the packet of heroin to STROMILE, STROMILE hands DENT the fifty bucks. After the exchange, DENT quickly grabs STROMILE's arm, stares at it for a moment, lets it fall. STROMILE exits.)

Scene Five

(Thursday. Evening)

(Apartment #5)

(A man is moaning in the dark. It is a deep, historical anguish.)

CARLOS: Stromile! ...Oh my god, Stromile! ...Jesus ...God help me... Our father who art in heaven hallowed be thy name they kingdom come thy will be done on earth as it is in heaven give us this day our daily bread... Stromile!... Somebody, please!

(The sound of a door opening, closing, quick footfalls.)

STROMILE: I'm here.

CARLOS: Thank god.

STROMILE: Lemme get the light.

(A light is turned on. A studio apartment is illuminated. It is beautifully decorated with antique furniture, stained glass Harlequin lamps, portraits of various black-and-white film actresses in ornate frames. CARLOS is in bed. He is early thirties, medically bald, covered with lesions. He is wearing white pajamas. He is severely frightened, breathing heavily.)

STROMILE: Can you see?

CARLOS: I can make out shapes. You wearin a blue shirt, right?

STROMILE: It's white.

CARLOS: I keep seein blue. Damn... I shit the bed again.

(STROMILE quickly exits and returns moments later with a damp wash cloth, a wet towel, and a plastic container of Babywipes. He folds the washcloth in thirds and places it over

CARLOS' *head. He then turns* CARLOS *on his side and starts to clean him.)*

CARLOS: I'm sorry, Stromile.

STROMILE: It's okay, Carlos. It's okay.

CARLOS: The pain...

STROMILE: Your legs again?

CARLOS: My legs, my arms, the soles of my feet.
Did you hear me, I was prayin and shit.

STROMILE: I heard you.

CARLOS: I haven't prayed since I was little. I can't believe that nonsense... I couldn't feel my legs earlier.

STROMILE: Can you feel em now?

CARLOS: Uh-huh. But they hurt so much.

STROMILE: You want your stuff?

CARLOS: Yeah, but you gonna have to help me again. I can't keep my hands from shaking.

(STROMILE *crosses to a bureau, opens a drawer, removes a works kit, returns to* CARLOS' *bed. From the kit,* STROMILE *produces a rubber tube, a capped syringe, a small knot of heroin, a spoon, a lighter.)*

CARLOS: Did you get the raw stuff or the China white?

STROMILE: I got the raw stuff.

CARLOS: Cause the raw stuff hits me good. The China white's like doin Sudafed...
   This heat. It's like dogs breathin on you...Stromile, you should wear those rubber gloves Mrs Palacios brought us.

STROMILE: Just get you a good vein.

(STROMILE *uncaps the syringe, cooks the heroine in the spoon, draws it into the syringe, tabs the bubbles out.)*

STROMILE: You don't got no more veins, Carlos. Where'd them shits go?

(STROMILE *sets the syringe between his teeth, fixes the rubber tube around* CARLOS' *arm.*)

STROMILE: You wanna skin pop?

CARLOS: No, I wanna shoot that shit.

STROMILE: Make a fist.

CARLOS: I can't.

STROMILE: Come on, Carlos, make a fist, yo.

(CARLOS *struggles to makes a fist, but does so.*)

STROMILE: Make another one.

(CARLOS *makes another fist, releases.* STROMILE *taps out a vein, and shoots the heroin into* CARLOS' *arm, empties the syringe, removes it, holds his arm for a moment, then unties the tube.* CARLOS *luxuriates in the rush while* STROMILE *places the works back in the kit, removes a plastic baggie, caps the needle, places it in the baggie.*)

(STROMILE *stares at the baggie for a moment, hides it under the bureau, then returns to* CARLOS, *where he continues to clean him in bed.*)

STROMILE: Well, you obviously ate.

CARLOS: *(Already high, giggling)* I was suddenly so hungry.

STROMILE: What'd you have?

CARLOS: Mrs Palacios brought me a Extra Value Meal. Two Cheeseburgers, large fry, Orange Fanta.

STROMILE: It was good, huh?

CARLOS: Oh, Papi, it was heaven.

STROMILE: I ain't your Papi.

CARLOS: I know. You my Stromile.

STROMILE: I ain't nobody's nothin. Let's get you outta those pajamas.

(He takes CARLOS' *pajamas off.)*

CARLOS: How can you stand to look at me. I'm so ugly.

*(*STROMILE *is all business.)*

CARLOS: You sposed to say "You ain't ugly, Carlos, you the bomb."..."You ain't ugly, Carlos, you the bomb."..."You ain't ugly, Carlos, you the bomb."

*(*STROMILE *puts the pajamas in a laundry bag, crosses to a bureau, opens the bottom drawer, holds up a few pairs of pajamas.)*

STROMILE: Green or red?

CARLOS: What about the purple ones?

STROMILE: You shit them joints.

CARLOS: I did?

STROMILE: Yeah, two days ago.

CARLOS: I feel green so I guess give me those.

*(*STROMILE *closes the bureau, crosses to* CARLOS *with the green pajamas, helps him into them.)*

CARLOS: Oh, I'm so disgusting. If I could speak Spanish I would say that shit in Spanish. Yo estoy mucho disgusto, or whatever.

STROMILE: You don't know Spanish?

CARLOS: Stromile, you been livin here for eight months. Have you ever heard me speak a syllable of Spanish?

STROMILE: I thought you was Puerto Rican.

CARLOS: Do I look Puerto Rican?

STROMILE: No, you look white, but you act Puerto Rican. And you got a Puerto Rican name.

CARLOS: I'm Scotch Irish and German.

STROMILE: Then how you get a name like Carlos?

CARLOS: Carlos ain't my real name.

STROMILE: It ain't?

CARLOS: Nuh-uh.

STROMILE: What is it?

CARLOS: I ain't tellin you.

STROMILE: Why not?

CARLOS: Cuz that shit is embarrassing.

STROMILE: Come on, Carlos, don't be a punk.

CARLOS: The past is the past, papi. *(Pause)* Okay, I'll tell you cause my ugly self ain't gonna be around much longer and for some reason I'm feeling sentimental. But you better not laugh.

STROMILE: I won't.

CARLOS: You gotta promise.

STROMILE: Just tell me.

CARLOS: Promise, Stromile.

STROMILE: I promise.

CARLOS: ...In my former life I was Larry. I was baptized Larry David Groom.

STROMILE: Larry David Groom?

CARLOS: Uh-huh.

STROMILE: Damn.

CARLOS: What?

STROMILE: It's just bug.

CARLOS: What's bug about it?

STROMILE: You just don't seem like no Larry.

CARLOS: I'm not Larry, I'm Carlos Castaneda Ortega. It's a dope name, right?

STROMILE: Yeah, that shit is kinda dope.... How old was you when you changed it?

CARLOS: Sixteen.

STROMILE: And all this time I thought you was Puerto Rican.

CARLOS: Trust me. I wish I was. All those Latin bulls from South Lock mighta took more of an interest in my pale ass. I had to settle for Brian Von Drasek and his U F O obsession... Poor sad little Brian. I wonder where that faggit is right now.

STROMILE: Please don't start sweatin that nigga again.

(Pause)

CARLOS: So whatchu do today?

STROMILE: I didn't do shit. Spent half the morning waitin for this knucklehead down by the river.

CARLOS: I still don't understand what it is that you do exactly.

STROMILE: I told you it ain't none of your business.

CARLOS: It is my business, Stromile. I promised your mother I would keep an eye on you.

STROMILE: Don't I know it.... I don't understand how you two became friends in the first place.

CARLOS: Why do you say that?

STROMILE: My moms hated Puerto Ricans.

CARLOS: But I ain't Puerto Rican. I just proved that.

STROMILE: She hated white people, too.

CARLOS: Well, it just goes to show you.

STROMILE: What.

CARLOS: A plague can inspire the most unlikely bonds of solidarity. Evie was my girl.

STROMILE: It's only cuz you both like them corny-ass disco records.

CARLOS: Oh, it is not, Stromile. She was a Virgo. We were astrologically compatible. She helped me through some very difficult shit. And now I'm helping you and you helping me. It's like one big beautiful buddy system, right?

STROMILE: Yeah, real beautiful.

(CARLOS is seized with pain. He grabs his legs. He cries out. STROMILE calms him, rubs his legs.)

CARLOS: I want to die, Stromile.

STROMILE: Release your legs.

(CARLOS howls out with pain.)

STROMILE: Your legs, Carlos! Release them joints! ...There you go.

(STROMILE continues working on his legs for a moment.)

CARLOS: *(Trying to relax)* I'm serious, Stromile. I want you to help me die. I can't stand it anymore. There are ways.

STROMILE: I'm callin the motherfuckin hospital.

CARLOS: *(Grabbing his arm)* Please, Stromile. A pillow over my face. In the middle of the night. It'll be like I went in my sleep. I'm almost totally blind. The pain is so big. Even when I'm high now. Two pillows. Nice and gentle. Please. We could do it this weekend.

STROMILE: Why don't you sing a song or some shit?

CARLOS: Oh, you such a little subject changer.

STROMILE: I'm serious.

CARLOS: I wrote a new one today. It came to me when that old man from across the courtyard was playing his trombone.

STROMILE: That nigga crazy.

CARLOS: It was so sad, Stromile. Like trees in winter or some shit. I got the trombone on tape. I was gonna play it back, but my hands... I couldn't press the buttons, no more.

STROMILE: You want me to press em for you?

CARLOS: Yes, please.

(STROMILE *crosses to the bureau, removes a fairly crude tape player, sets it on the bed in front of* CARLOS.)

CARLOS: I'm serious, Stromile. You can help me.

STROMILE: I don't wanna talk about that shit right now.

CARLOS: Okay, but at some point we need to talk about it. Just think: I'll be out of pain and you won't have to worry about my ass no more and you'll meet a beautiful Nubian princess and take her to a tropical island and eat her pussy in some little bungalow by the sea.

STROMILE: I don't eat pussy.

CARLOS: Then you can eat her butthole.

(STROMILE *protests.*)

CARLOS: Oh, you a freak and you know it.

(Pause)

STROMILE: I ain't gonna never meet no beautiful Nubian princess.

CARLOS: You never know.

STROMILE: Ain't nothin round here but hoes and crackheads. Wack-ass Gompers.

CARLOS: You gotta be patient.

STROMILE: Patience don't do nothin but make you old.

CARLOS: What you need to do is stop wearin those white T-shirts. You look like you A-WOL or some shit.

STROMILE: I don't got nothin better.

CARLOS: Go open my bottom drawer.

STROMILE: Why?

CARLOS: Just do it.

(STROMILE *crosses to the bureau, opens the bottom drawer, pulls out a gift box.*)

STROMILE: What's this?

CARLOS: It's a gift.

STROMILE: A gift?

CARLOS: A token of my thanks. Just open it.

(STROMILE *opens it. It's a blue shirt with a collar.*)

STROMILE: Where'd you get this?

CARLOS: I ordered it out of a catalog. Mrs Palacios Helped me. It's blue, right?

STROMILE: Yeah, it's blue.

CARLOS: Put it on.

(STROMILE *puts it on.* CARLOS *strains to see him.*)

STROMILE: Do it look gay?

CARLOS: Stromile you couldn't look gay if you wanted to.... It's nice, right?

STROMILE: It's straight.

CARLOS: Come here.

STROMILE: Why?

CARLOS: Just come here. I can't see it so let me touch it.

(STROMILE *moves closer to him.* CARLOS *feels the material on the shirt.*)

CARLOS: Yeah, that shit is definitely blue. *(He retracts his hand.)* Wear that next time you go searchin for your Nubian princess. I guarantee success.

(STROMILE *looks at himself in the mirror for another moment.*)

STROMILE: Thanks, Carlos.

CARLOS: You welcome.

(STROMILE *takes the shirt off, puts it back in the box.*)

CARLOS: One more thing, Stromile.

STROMILE: What.

CARLOS: Promise me that after I pass you'll leave this place.

STROMILE: Leave Gompers?

CARLOS: Yes, papi, leave. This is a dead town. It ain't gonna do nothin but pull you under. I got some money saved for you. It's in a coffee can underneath the sink in the kitchen. It should be enough to get you set up for a coupla months.

STROMILE: Where am I sposed to go?

CARLOS: That's up to you. There's lots of places. Somewhere that ain't gonna drag you down. Somewhere that's gotta good public school so you can get your diploma.

STROMILE: I'm through with school. That shit is wack.

CARLOS: You not a dropout, Stromile! I won't be able to rest with that on my head... Promise me you'll take the money and start over somewhere, Stromile.

STROMILE: Okay, Carlos. Damn.

CARLOS: Give me your word.

STROMILE: I give you my word. You ready to sing?

(CARLOS nods.)

(STROMILE presses record on the cassette player. A distant trombone plays for a measure or two and then CARLOS starts to sing.)

CARLOS: *(Singing)* Flying monkeys
Dropping pennies from the sky
Cloud formations
Golden raindrops in your eye
Lonesome cowgirl
Lasso flying through the air
Herd the bovines
The butcher's waiting in the square

Where's the weather from last Sunday?
Where's the water in the bay?
The circus sold the bearded lady
And April lost three days to May

It's a lonely time for loving
All the schoolboys left in June
The Sheriff's eating taffy apples
Let's go paint the jailhouse blue
Let's go paint the jailhouse blue

Oh yes, the crowd is fully gathered
The preacher dons his Sunday clothes
When the stuntman sets the record
I'll gladly throw the final rose
I'll gladly throw the final rose...

(CARLOS leans back, nods off, too high to finish the song.)

(STROMILE keeps him from falling off the bed. He holds him for a moment, then tucks him in, as the trombone continues to play on the tape recorder.)

Scene Six

(Thursday. Evening)

(The waterfront)

(On the picnic table there is an empty forty ounce bottle of Old English 800, some broken glass.)

(WHITE STEVE runs with his sword, slides on his knees. He is exhilarated. He removes a cell phone from his pocket, looks at it, turns it in the moonlight, attempting to figure out how to turn it on. He figures it out. It bleeps a few bleeps. He dials a number, waits.)

WHITE STEVE: Hello?... Hey, Chuckie... What's up, yo?... It's Steve.... Chillin... I'm in Paris.... Yep, Paris, France. You should see all the bitches they got here. Polly voo Transam and all that... You seen Junie?... Yeah?... She's still lookin good, huh?... Yeah, I'll be back someday, too much business right now... Thanks, kid... Hey, I gotta go... Aaight.

(MOLLY emerges from the shadows, watches him, undetected.)

(WHITE STEVE hangs up, dials another number.)

WHITE STEVE: Yo, Straw, what's up moneyman?... Chillin, chillin... You still stylin and profilin?... Yeah?... Yeah?... Aw snap!... Oh, I'm down in Mexico... Mexico City. You should see all the honeys down here... Yeah, freaky banditas... There's this one girl called Vanessa. She's got three titties.... Word is bond, B! She let's me sleep on the middle one.... Hey, I gotta go. You see Skram tell his ass he still owes me that money... Okay, I'm out.

(WHITE STEVE hangs up, dials again.)

WHITE STEVE: Hey, Ma, it's Steve... Hey... Good...
Gompers... Yeah, that juvy hotel couldn't keep me as
long as they wanted... Yeah, I'm in school.... Geometry,
History, Zoology, stuff like that. Yesterday we drew a
llama... Yeah, I drew mines pretty good, but I got in
trouble cuz I drew his nuts too big.... I know.... *(He starts
to cry)* So if I came home for a while would that be
cool?... Uh-huh... Uh-huh... I won't.... I'll be good....
Has daddy been by?... He is?... He got a new tattoo?
Where?... What is it?... Cool... Okay... Yeah, I'm really
comin home.... In a few weeks... Me too.

(WHITE STEVE hangs up, wipes his face, sees MOLLY.)

MOLLY: Where'd you get that?

WHITE STEVE: What?

MOLLY: That cell phone. Where'd you get it?

WHITE STEVE: I just got it.

MOLLY: They don't work here yet.

WHITE STEVE: Yes they do.

MOLLY: No they don't. Ebony Bunch tried to use one
yesterday.

WHITE STEVE: Well, it works now cuz I was just talkin
on it.

MOLLY: No you weren't.

WHITE STEVE: Yes I was.

MOLLY: You were just playin. It's okay, I do it, too.
(She produces a pack of Merits.) Want one?

WHITE STEVE: I thought you quit.

MOLLY: I did, but sometimes I still carry em around.
Want one or not?

WHITE STEVE: Yeah.

(She proffers the cigarettes. He takes two, puts one behind his ear. MOLLY *produces a lighter, lights him.)*

MOLLY: So, Steve, where do you sleep, anyway?

WHITE STEVE: Why, you wanna sleep with me?

MOLLY: Seriously. You don't got a home, do you?

WHITE STEVE: I don't need no home.

MOLLY: You think you're so tough. You're just a little boy.

WHITE STEVE: Yeah, I'll show you how little.

MOLLY: You smoke like you think you're in a movie or somethin.

WHITE STEVE: Maybe I am. Maybe they're filmin that shit right now. *(He gives an invisible camera man the finger, smokes, grabs the bottle of Old English 800.)* Wish I had some brew. Mickeys. How come they don't sell no Mickeys around here?

MOLLY: There's a lot of stuff they don't sell around here... Gompers used to have a mall. There was this fountain in the middle. People would throw pennies in it. And there was this video arcade called Aladdin's Castle. And a food court with a Sbarro's pizza. But it closed. But now they got that gambling boat coming. I'm gonna try and get a job on it.

WHITE STEVE: A job doin what?

MOLLY: Dealin blackjack.

WHITE STEVE: What do you know about blackjack?

MOLLY: I know about it. Doublin down and low Chicago and all that. My mom taught me.

WHITE STEVE: I heard your moms is a junky hoe.

MOLLY: She's not a junky, Steve, she's an alcoholic. And she's not a hoe, either. She used to do the books at the Steel Mill.

WHITE STEVE: Ebony Bunch told me she fucked your softball coach at parent teacher conferences. That you walked in on her lickin his nuts. Ebony Bunch said she was lit.

MOLLY: Everyone makes mistakes, Steve. Besides, she stopped drinkin. She found god.

WHITE STEVE: Where'd she find him, at the car wash?

MOLLY: She just found him. Like in her heart. You know what a heart is?

(Pause)

WHITE STEVE: I wouldn't wanna work on no boat.

MOLLY: Why not?

WHITE STEVE: I don't know. What if it sinks or somethin? That's what I'm scaredest of.

MOLLY: What?

WHITE STEVE: Drownin. Drownin and gettin poisoned. I'd rather get capped in the head.

MOLLY: Steve, how old are you, anyway?

WHITE STEVE: Old enough.

MOLLY: No, really, how old?

WHITE STEVE: Seventeen.

MOLLY: No you're not!

WHITE STEVE: Fourteen.

MOLLY: You're still lyin.

WHITE STEVE: Thirteen. But I'll be fourteen in August.

MOLLY: Where'd you live before you came to Gompers?

WHITE STEVE: In this juvy hotel.

MOLLY: You were at Hamstock?

WHITE STEVE: I was in Hefty.

MOLLY: What's Hefty?

WHITE STEVE: Home Environment for Troubled Youths.

MOLLY: Where's that?

WHITE STEVE: South Lock.

MOLLY: Is that where you're from?

WHITE STEVE: Hey, guess what?

MOLLY: What?

WHITE STEVE: I know how to get this big-ass trombone, wanna buy it?

MOLLY: No.

WHITE STEVE: I'll sell it to you cheap.

MOLLY: What would I do with a trombone?

WHITE STEVE: I don't know. Play it. It's all shiny. Crisper than icebird lettuce. (He stops smoking, stares out at the water.) Oh, snap!

MOLLY: What?

WHITE STEVE: I thought I just saw somethin.

MOLLY: What?

WHITE STEVE: This man on the water. He was like fishin or some shit.... He ain't there no more.

MOLLY: It's prolly just your mind playin tricks on you.

WHITE STEVE: No, I saw it, Molly! I swear I saw it! He was blue!

MOLLY: Really?

WHITE STEVE: I ain't lyin!

(MOLLY *starts to slowly back away.*)

WHITE STEVE: Where you goin?

MOLLY: I gotta go help my mom. I promised her I'd be home early tonight. But it was nice talking to you, Steve. (*She backs into the darkness.*)

(WHITE STEVE *stares out at the water.*)

WHITE STEVE: (*To the water*) Yo!... Yo, Mister! You wanna buy a trombone? (*He stares out at the water, confused. After a moment, he sits and smokes.*)

END OF ACT ONE

ACT TWO

Scene One

(Saturday morning)

(The kitchen of the courtyard apartment)

(The walls are adorned with war paraphernalia: pennants, flags, mounted weapons, etc. On the floor, several bundled stacks of old newspapers, phone books, and scattered racing forms. The kitchen table is covered with an American Flag. On top of the table, an old trombone.)

(NEIL FINN, mid-to-late-seventies, white, is carefully setting a chair next to the table. He wears dress greens with impeccably shined shoes. His coat is carefully arranged with various ribbons and medals. His hair is combed severely. He is holding a noose. He drapes the flag over his trombone ceremoniously, steps onto the chair, secures his balance, then steps on the center of the table, straddling the trombone. He gathers himself and then attempts to secure the free end of the noose to a hook that had once held a light fixture.)

(A knock on the door)

(FINN turns to the door, waits.)

(Another knock)

DENT: Mr Finn...

(FINN gets down off the table, opens a drawer, hides the noose.)

DENT: Mr Finn, it's your super, Richard Dent. I gotta talk to you.

(FINN *opens the drawer, removes the noose, stuffs it into the cupboard under the sink.*)

DENT: Mr Finn, I can hear you shufflin around in there.

FINN: I paid the rent!

DENT: I know you paid your rent, Mr Finn.

FINN: I pay it on the first of the month! Ninety-four dollars and thirty-seven cents! Ninety-four thirty-seven!

DENT: This concerns another matter, Mr Finn.

FINN: I've been livin in this building since 1961. I haven't been late in forty-three years! Go away!

DENT: Mr Finn, I promise you it's about somethin else... I'll key in if I have to.

(FINN *crosses to the door, opens it.* DENT *and* NOLAN *stand in the entrance. They are wearing respectable clothes: slacks, decent shoes, sport jackets.*)

FINN: What do you want?

DENT: May we come in, please?

FINN: I'm busy.

DENT: Mr Finn, this won't take long, I promise.

(FINN *steps aside. They enter.*)

NOLAN: Hey, Mr Finn. (*He takes a seat at the kitchen table.*)

DENT: You're looking very sharp today, Mr Finn. What's the occasion?

FINN: Occasion? I was a Major in the United States Army, that's the occasion. I have every right to wear my dress greens.

DENT: Fair enough... That's fair, right, Nolan?

NOLAN: Sure.

FINN: *(To* DENT*)* What does he know?

NOLAN: What.

FINN: *(To* DENT*)* I've never seen such a sweet potato. *(To* NOLAN*).* Peel the skin off and look what's underneath. Yankee-doodle in a flower patch. Should make you clean the latrine. Next time bring your toothbrush.

DENT: Take a seat, Mr Finn.

FINN: Why?

DENT: So we can have a conversation.

FINN: I don't wanna sit.

DENT: Come on, Mr Finn, there's no pressure here. Take a load off. Let's be civil.

FINN: You tryin to say I'm not a citizen? I fought in a war, Mister! Took a bullet in a very private place! Very private! Got medals for valor and courage! You're outta line, soldier!

DENT: Mr Finn, there's no need to fly off the handle. We're here with the best intentions. We just want to clear some things up is all.

FINN: *(Referring to* NOLAN*)* I don't trust that guy. Him and his play partner rollin in the ivy. *(To* NOLAN*)* Do you even work?

NOLAN: I used to.

DENT: Mr Finn, Nolan worked for the steel mill. He was a lableman, right Nolan?

NOLAN: Ladleman.

DENT: I mean ladleman. Since they shut down he's been helping me out around the building.

FINN: He ain't been preserving the species, I'll tell you that much.

DENT: Mr Finn, this would be so much easier if we were all sitting.

FINN: I don't wanna sit. Where's my saber, anyway? Eyes right, ready front. Eyes right... Someone keeps screwin with my stuff.

(DENT *crosses to* FINN, *guides him to the table.*)

FINN: What!... I didn't do nothin! I pay my rent on time! I take my trash to the curb...

DENT: Take it easy, Mr Finn.

(DENT *gently seats him in a chair.* DENT *sits as well. All three are seated at the table now.*)

DENT: There, that's better, right? How bout somethin to drink? You thirsty, Mr Finn?

FINN: No.

DENT: You sure?

FINN: Why would I be thirsty? Do I look thirsty?

DENT: I'm just tryin to be hospitable. It's hot out there today. Sposed to get in the nineties.

FINN: This is my apartment, Mister. I don't care who you are. I got my own chain of command here and I decide when it's time to call the goddamn hospital.

DENT: I'll get to the point.

FINN: I would.... (*Looking at* NOLAN) Somebody should stick a pin in Private Sweet Potato over here. (*To* NOLAN) You know what they do to sweet potatoes in the Army, Private? They mash em up and serve em to the commies and the krauts.

DENT: Mr Finn, please.

FINN: Feed the whole lot of em.

DENT: Mr Finn, in the past few days I've fielded several complaints regarding your trombone playing.

FINN: You fielded who?

DENT: Complaints.

FINN: I painted these walls ten years ago. Double primed em and everything.

DENT: COMPLAINTS, Mr Finn, not PAINT. I've fielded COMPLAINTS.

FINN: I can't stand complainers. I say put em all on a pontoon boat and let it drift out to sea. The complainers and the yellow bellies. Mommy criers, all of em.

DENT: Mr Finn, they were complaining about your trombone playing.

FINN: My what?

DENT: YOUR TROMBONE PLAYING.

FINN: Who was complaining?

DENT: I've received two phone calls and several notes.

FINN: Notes, what kinda notes?

DENT: Written notes.

FINN: From who?

DENT: That's not important.

FINN: It is so important! Stuff gets put in code, and someone's gotta decipher it. Send it over to H Q so the boys in Intelligence can get a move on. We live in desperate times, Mister. Desperate, desperate times. ALPHA. BRAVO. FOXTROT. ECHO. DOUBLE HOTEL. DOUBLE DELTA. CHARLIE IN THE APPLE GROVE. GOATS AND MONKEYS, GOATS AND MONKEYS! There's a code right there. Did you hear it?

DENT: These notes are not in code, Mr Finn, I assure
you.

FINN: Well, what do they say?

DENT: It's confidential.

FINN: Who's congressional?

DENT: CONFIDENTIAL. I'm not at liberty to discuss
their contents.

FINN: Oh, what the hell do you know about liberty?

DENT: Mr Finn—

FINN: Liberty and justice for all. Now there's a code.
It sounds like one thing but sometimes it means a world
of hurt. You ever seen our flag with scrambled eggs and
ketchup on it?

DENT: Mr Finn, I don't think we're communicating very
well.

FINN: Well, that's your problem. I talk to people all the
time. Talk to em on the street. Talk to em on the phone.
I've written thousands of letters in my day. Letters
to my congressman. Letters to the Pope. Letters to
the president of the United States of America, the
Commander in Chief. Literally thousands of hand-
written letters. Do you know what the definition of
leadership is? It's the process in which you influence
others to accomplish a mission. Leadership takes
communication skills. I was a Major in the United States
Army. I fought in a war on a dark continent and won
various medals and ribbons. Commendations galore.
They don't just throw Valor and Courage around like
they're sticks in a wagon. I carried a saber. I had a
mountain of men under me. A mountain of trained
soldiers. Don't talk to me about communication, Mister.

DENT: I'll put it bluntly, Mr Finn: You can't play your trombone in the courtyard at seven-thirty in the morning. It's not fair to the other tenants.

FINN *starts to put the trombone in its case.*

FINN: No one has any pride any more. No pride and no guts. What happened to this country anyway? Used to be you could get people excited about things. Start a rally. Pump your fist in the air. Now it's all stuffed cabbage and cream corn. *(To* NOLAN, *putting the case under the table)* I know what you're about, Sweet Potato. Don't think I don't know. You belong in the funny barracks. *(To* DENT*)* Don't drop your soap around him.

DENT: Mr Finn, are we in agreement about your trombone playing or not?

FINN: What?

DENT: YOUR TROMBONE PLAYING. DO YOU UNDERSTAND THAT YOU CAN'T PLAY SO EARLY IN THE MORNING.

FINN: But I gotta practice.

DENT: Practice for what?

FINN: I'm in a band. I'm First Trombone.

DENT: What band?

FINN: The V F W band. We got a parade comin up. Knights of Columbus and the V F W. Straight down Jefferson. They're blockin off the whole street and we're goin right over the bridge. When the Saint's Go Marchin in. Onward Christian Soldiers. Roll Out the Barrell. Lucy in the Sky with Nylons.

DENT: Mr Finn, I appreciate that you need to practice for this parade thing, but you gotta take into account that other people live in the building.

FINN: What about my hot water?! How come I don't got no hot water?! And I still can't open the window in Sally's room! Thing's been stuck for damn near twenty years now! *(He slams his fists onto the table.)*

DENT: Take it easy, Mr Finn.

FINN: Major Finn to you, recruit!

DENT: Take it easy, Major Finn.

(Awkward pause)

NOLAN: *(Moving things along)* Wow. It's really hot in here.

DENT: *(Playing along)* It sure is. And it's important to stay hydrated. Maybe Major Finn would like a glass of water. Would you like a glass of water, Major Finn?

FINN: I don't drink water. All the water in this town's contaminated with cowardice and stupidity. You get a good look at the river lately? It's all refinery runoff. *(To NOLAN)* You boys at the Steel Mill don't know how to dump your hogwash. It's about time they closed you down. I'd rather drink outta the latrine. And what the hell does hydrogen have to do with anything?

DENT: Major Finn, how bout some O J—you like O J? A little vitamin C to get those juices flowin.

FINN: Juices? What juices? *(Pointing to NOLAN)* He's the one who likes it juicy. That one there. Fat and juicy like a Christmas ham...

DENT: Whattaya like to drink, sir?

FINN: I drink Maxwell House. Maxwell House coffee.

DENT: Cream and sugar?

FINN: I take mine black. Black coffee's all I drink.

DENT: Nolan, make the Major a nice pot of coffee.
(To FINN*)* Maybe we'll join you for a cup of coffee.
Would you mind if we joined you, Major Finn?

FINN: I don't care what you join.

*(*NOLAN *crosses to the kitchen counter, locates the coffee maker, plugs it in. starts to open drawers and look for filters, the coffee, etc. He opens the cupboard under the sink, pulls out the noose, stares at it for a moment, hides it in the small of his back. He eventually locates the coffee and filters, starts to brew a pot of coffee.)*

DENT: So what are you up to these days, Major Finn?

FINN: What?

DENT: What have you been up to?

FINN: I understand about twenty percent of what's comin outta your mouth, Mister. What did you say your name was?

DENT: Richard.

FINN: I had a cat named Richard once. Richard the Cat. He was a Siamese and he crapped all over the place. Couldn't find the litter box if you hit him in the head with it. He thought he was invincible, too.... What was your question again?

DENT: I asked you what you've been doin to occupy your time. I mean, besides playing your trombone in the courtyard.

FINN: I'm a retired Major in the United States Army. I don't do nothin. I did several tours of duty. I've led thousands of men and I've earned my time to rest.

DENT: Do you have any hobbies?

FINN: I mostly just sit here. Right here like we're doin now. I'll occasionally thumb through the phone book. Make an important call or two. Why?

DENT: Just curious. I mean, we've been neighbors for almost fifteen years and I don't know much about you.

FINN: What's there to know?

DENT: General stuff. I mean, don't you wonder about the other people who live in this building? How they spend their days? What they do in the privacy of their own apartments?

FINN: If you're lookin to confess somethin I'd advise a visit to the base chaplain.

DENT: I'm serious, Major Finn. Do you have any family?

FINN: Sally and I had a daughter.

DENT: Where is she?

FINN: She's not anywhere.

DENT: Does she live in Gompers?

FINN: She died when she was still in diapers.

DENT: I'm sorry to hear that. What was her name?

FINN: I don't know. Somethin girly.

DENT: How'd she die?

FINN: She fell off the table. Right where you're sittin. Fell on her head and broke her neck. 1963. I was in the bathroom fixin a drip in the faucet. I heard the break. Sounded like a bird hittin the window. Sally never got over it. I kept telling her to move on, keep fightin, dig into the trench, but it ate her up.

DENT: What happened to Sally?

FINN: They had to take her away.

DENT: Who?

FINN: The folks from the mental hospital. She wouldn't stop cuttin herself. Blood all over the kitchen. Nothin but gore. Few years later she died.

DENT: How'd she die?

FINN: I don't know. Some such catastrophe or other.

DENT: I'm sorry to hear that, Major Finn.

FINN: We all dwindle to dust like dogs in the night.

DENT: Who said that?

FINN: What?

DENT: "We all dwindle to dust like dogs in the night."
Someone said that.

FINN: I said it.

DENT: But it's a quote, right. You like borrowed it.

FINN: I didn't borrow nothin. Last thing I borrowed was
a horse with a bad leg and that didn't get me anywhere.

DENT: Well, it's a very eloquent thing to say, Major Finn.

FINN: You callin me an elephant?

DENT: What? No. I said.... Forget it.

*(Behind them, NOLAN pours three cups of coffee. He then
removes the vial that WHITE STEVE had given to STROMILE
in ACT ONE, Scene Two. NOLAN unscrews the top and
pours its contents into one of the cups.)*

DENT: Nolan, how's the coffee comin?

NOLAN: It's comin.

*(NOLAN conceals the vial, then brings three coffee cups to the
table, sets one in front of DENT, one for himself, and one in
front of FINN, sits.)*

DENT: So you're a veteran, right Major Finn?

FINN: That's right.

DENT: What war were you in?

FINN: I fought in Korea.

DENT: How long were you over there?

FINN: Too long.

DENT: Where were you stationed?

FINN: Okinawa at first. But we were all over the place. Pyongyang. The Pusan perimeter. Seoul. The hills outside Taegu. Kunari.

(*Suddenly,* NOLAN *switches* DENT'*s coffee with* FINN'*s.*)

FINN: What do you think you're doin?

NOLAN: I forgot you took your coffee black, Mr Finn. This one's got sugar in it.

FINN: You like it sweet, huh?

NOLAN: Sure.

FINN: Yeah, I'll bet you do. (*He starts to drink from his coffee cup, stops.*) I can't figure out what happened to my damn saber. I just had it cleaned and mounted. It was hangin right there on the wall two days ago. Eyes right, ready front. Eyes right...

(DENT *starts to drink from his coffee cup.* NOLAN *stops him.*)

NOLAN: It's, um, too hot, Dent. Let it cool off a bit.

(DENT *sets his cup down. He and* NOLAN *share a look.*)

DENT: So, uh, Major Finn, what was it like in Korea?

FINN: What was it like?

DENT: Yeah, generally speaking. As in the weather, for instance. Was it hot?

FINN: Hot?! I spent the coldest damn winter of my life there! Thirty below zero sometimes. One night when the Chinks had us on our heels we marched across the Han River. Marched right across it like it was a block of concrete. Damn thing was frozen solid. One fella was so cold he started having visions. Kept thinkin he was seein Jesus ice skating.

DENT: Wow.

FINN: Jesus Christola himself. Doin figure eights right there on the Han River.

NOLAN: Was he blue?

FINN: Was Jesus a Jew? Of course he was a Jew! Jesus was king of that bunch! What the hell does that have to do with anything?!

DENT: Major Finn, what's the Silver Star for?

FINN: Gallantry.

DENT: How'd you get that?

FINN: Get it? It was awarded to me. I led a platoon of flesh-and-blood infantrymen against five North Korean T-34 tanks. Destroyed three of them with frost-bitten soldiers and a pretty feeble collection of Springfield rifles. Spit and toilet paper went a long way back then.

DENT: Did you get shot?

FINN: I took more bullets than most people got teeth... You haven't touched your coffee, Rodney.

DENT: Richard. It's still too hot.

(FINN *reaches across the table and seizes* DENT's *coffee cup, drinks the whole cup very quickly.*)

FINN: Hot? That wasn't hot. It was practically room temperature. (*To* NOLAN) What about you, Snowflake?

NOLAN: I sorta lost my thirst.

FINN: Lost your thirst?! How the hell does that happen?

DENT: Major Finn, Nolan recently sustained some very serious abdominal wounds and his appetite's been a little unpredictable.

FINN: Pass it over here then. No need to waste a good cup of Maxwell House.

(NOLAN *passes his coffee cup to* FINN, *who drains it very quickly, sets it down.*)

FINN: I thought you said you put sugar in that?

NOLAN: I did.

FINN: Didn't taste sweet to me.

NOLAN: Maybe it was flour.

FINN: I'll show you a flower.

(FINN *and* DENT *share laughter.*)

FINN: I used to drink nine, ten cups of coffee in a row. Brew up a pot, get another one ready—Major Finn's in town. Eyes right, ready front! Dig it in, boys!

DENT: *(Referring to his coffee)* What about yours, Major Finn?

FINN: My damn coffee cup smells like two-day-old trout. *(he smells it)* What the hell, that's never stopped me before. Here's to Bravo Company....

(FINN *starts to drink. An urgent knock on the door. He puts the cup down.*)

SHOE: Mr Finn, it's Julius Shoe from the second floor.

FINN: Go away, I got company!

SHOE: Mr Finn, I don't mean to bother you and I apologize in advance for the inconvenience, but is the super in there by any chance?

DENT: Later, Shoe!

SHOE: Dent, I gotta talk to you. It's VERY IMPORTANT.

DENT: Major Finn, would you mind if I answered the door? I apologize for the interruption.

FINN: Suit yourself.

(DENT *crosses to the door, opens it.* SHOE *is there, looking a little freaked out.*)

SHOE: Hey, Nolan. Hey, Mr Finn. Sorry to interrupt.

DENT: What's up, Shoe?

SHOE: The box is gone.

DENT: What?

SHOE: Apache was here and he wanted to see you so I keyed into your apartment—

DENT: You keyed into my apartment?! *(To* FINN*)* Excuse me Major Finn. *(To* SHOE*)* You keyed into my fuckin apartment?!

SHOE: I can explain.

DENT: That key is to be used for emergencies only.

SHOE: This seemed like an emergency. Dent, I knocked like twenty times. Apache was really anxious to see you.

DENT: Great.

SHOE: Anyway, your bedroom window was wide open and the box was gone. I wanted to tell you as soon as possible.

DENT: The box is gone?

SHOE: Gone.

DENT: Fuck me... Nolan, we gotta go.

(NOLAN *rises, crosses to the door.*)

DENT: Major Finn, it was nice visiting with you. Enjoy the rest of your coffee.

(DENT, NOLAN, *and* SHOE *exit.* FINN *sits there staring at the cup of coffee. He grabs it, lifts it to his face, smells it, sets it down, reaches under the table and pulls out the trombone case, removes the trombone. He tries to play it, stops. He weeps. He sets the trombone on the table, rises, crosses to the sink, opens the cupboard underneath, roots through it for the noose, closes the cupboard, looks around confusedly, slowly exits to the back of the apartment.)*

Scene Two

(Saturday night)

(The train bridge. Fireworks exploding)

(MOLLY is sitting in the middle of the bridge, her legs dangling over the edge. She is looking around, waiting. She is holding a fresh pack of Merits. She periodically packs them against the back of her wrist. Fireworks are exploding over the river. STROMILE appears. He is wearing the blue shirt that CARLOS gave him.)

STROMILE: What's up?

MOLLY: Hey.

STROMILE: How long you been here?

MOLLY: Since nine.

STROMILE: You alone?

MOLLY: Uh-huh.

STROMILE: You sure?

MOLLY: I'm positive.

STROMILE: There's mad niggas down at the waterfront.

MOLLY: Yeah, I saw.... I like your shirt.

STROMILE: You do?

MOLLY: Yeah, that color's good on you.

STROMILE: Do it make me look gay?

MOLLY: Nu-uh. Far from it.

STROMILE: Cool.

MOLLY: Look at the water. It's so black it's like it's not even there. When the fireworks explode they look like stars. Like we're on the other side of the sky.

(They watch the reflection of the fireworks on the water.)

MOLLY: You can come stand next to me. I don't bite.

(He stands next to her, point at her cigarettes.)

STROMILE: You can't be smokin squares with a baby in you, Molly.

MOLLY: I know.

STROMILE: That joint'll shrivel up and fall out.

(MOLLY puts the cigarettes in her pocket.)

MOLLY: Hey, hold my hand.

STROMILE: Molly...

MOLLY: Please?

(He takes her hand tentatively. They watch the fireworks for a moment. Distant cheers from the waterfront.)

STROMILE: If Dent sees this that nigga'll kill me.

MOLLY: He's not gonna see it.

STROMILE: What if he comes up here?

MOLLY: I promise he won't.

STROMILE: You know he got a gat.

MOLLY: So?

STROMILE: So it ain't no squirt gun.

(MOLLY kisses him. It's a good kiss. They sit in silence.)

STROMILE: ...Damn.

MOLLY: What.

STROMILE: Just damn.

MOLLY: I've wanted to do that for a long time.

STROMILE: Really?

MOLLY: Uh-huh. There's somethin about you, Stromile.

STROMILE: There is?

MOLLY: Definitely. I used to watch you in Social Studies.

STROMILE: You did?

MOLLY: Yep. Biology, too.

STROMILE: What would you watch?

MOLLY: Just you. The way you'd walk into class.

STROMILE: How do I walk into class?

MOLLY: Tryin to be all cool like you have a limp.

STROMILE: I wasn't tryin to be cool! I sprained my ankle!

MOLLY: Yeah, right.

STROMILE: I did it playin ball in Gym. That shit was sore for like two months.

MOLLY: Uh-huh... You used to watch me, too.

STROMILE: You trippin, Molly.

MOLLY: I'm not stupid, Stromile. I could feel it.

(He takes his hand back.)

STROMILE: So how the baby doin, anyway?

MOLLY: Good.

STROMILE: You still eatin black licorice.

MOLLY: I got some in my bag. Wanna piece?

STROMILE: That shit is nasty.

MOLLY: I'm into cheese and jelly sandwiches now, too. And Cinnamon Toast Crunch... Ricky doesn't want me to have it. He keeps callin it a liability.

STROMILE: A liability?

MOLLY: Like it's car insurance or somethin. *(She takes out her pack of Merits, removes the plastic, peels away the foil, considers them a moment, puts them back in her pocket.)* Ebony Bunch was tellin me how you can make yourself have a miscarriage by drinking this blue stuff and having someone hit you in the stomach with a hammer.

STROMILE: What blue stuff?

MOLLY: Just this stuff. I don't know what it's called. You can get it in South Lock.

STROMILE: How the fuck do she know about that?

MOLLY: She did it.

STROMILE: When?

MOLLY: Last year.

STROMILE: She was pregnant?

MOLLY: Yeah, but nobody knew. She hid it with baggy clothes. She was almost four months into it when she did it.

STROMILE: Who was the father?

MOLLY: Dougie Dyd's cousin.

STROMILE: Shine?!

MOLLY: Yep.

STROMILE: That wack nigga?!

MOLLY: Ebony Bunch liked him.

STROMILE: Yeah, she gave up that pussy cuz he had a gold tooth and some nice kicks. His breath stank like dog-do. Basic-ass gang banger.
  I'm tired of these niggas comin to Gompers, gettin some ass, pissin in the river, and leavin like they doin us some kinda favor.... Do that bitch know you pregnant?

MOLLY: Yep.

STROMILE: Then why the fuck would she tell you about somethin like that?

MOLLY: I asked her.

STROMILE: You asked her?

MOLLY: Uh-huh.

STROMILE: You was just curious, huh?

MOLLY: You think about stuff, you know? The options. She still had some of the blue stuff. She gave it to me.... (*From her pocket she removes a glass bottle containing a blue liquid.*) But I'm having the baby.

(*She puts the bottle back her pocket. More fireworks*)

MOLLY: Mrs Palacios was telling my mom how the government likes single mothers.

STROMILE: What do she know?

MOLLY: She's old, Stromile. She knows stuff.

STROMILE: Mrs Palacios been on welfare longer than we been alive.

MOLLY: She was sayin that single mothers can get all this financial aide for college. If I get into G C C I can practically go for free.

STROMILE: You goin to G C C?

MOLLY: I want to.

STROMILE: Why?

MOLLY: So I can get a degree. Have a future.

STROMILE: What you gonna study?

MOLLY: Business Administration.

STROMILE: To do what?

MOLLY: I don't know. Administrate business.

STROMILE: College is wack, Molly.

MOLLY: Why do you say that?

STROMILE: Don't nobody learn nothin. It's where white people go to drink beer.

MOLLY: Black people drink beer, too, Stromile... You should go to college.

STROMILE: Fuck that.

MOLLY: Stromile, you could be anything you want.

STROMILE: Now you sound like that guidance counselor—Mrs Kimshits.

MOLLY: Kleinshmidt.

STROMILE: Yeah, her. Always tryin to get niggas amped about college. Apply to this school. Apply to that one. Take the S A T. Take that shit twice. Don't try and answer the ones you don't know. It's all bullshit.

MOLLY: Stromile, You were the smartest person in biology.

STROMILE: Stop lyin.

MOLLY: You were. After you left, Mr Prisby talked about you like you were some kinda legend.

STROMILE: That's just cuz didn't nobody else give a fuck.

MOLLY: I did.

STROMILE: Yeah, you, me and those two sisters with the neck braces.

MOLLY: The Hertzberger twins. They're so geeky.

STROMILE: They smart as hell.

MOLLY: How come you stopped comin?

STROMILE: I just did.

MOLLY: Why?

STROMILE: You always gotta be gettin up in my business, don't you, Molly?

MOLLY: I wish you would tell me.

STROMILE: I can't.

MOLLY: Why not?

STROMILE: I just can't, okay?

MOLLY: Tell me, Stromile. I promise I won't ask any more questions.

STROMILE: Molly George not ask a question?

MOLLY: I swear I won't.

STROMILE: Aiight, I'll tell you. But keep this shit between you and me. I don't need Ebony Bunch and all them waterfront hoes bumpin at the gums about my business.

MOLLY: It'll be our secret.

STROMILE: Last year after my moms passed, I moved in with this dude Carlos. Everbody know him as Carlos the Queer.

MOLLY: I know Carlos. He lives across the courtyard.

STROMILE: Well, now I live there, too.

MOLLY: You do?

STROMILE: Yeah. My moms and Carlos was in this support group for people with H I V and shit. They got real tight. He helped her a lot after she was doin chemo. He would sing songs and read her the newspaper and shit.

Before my moms passed she signed these papers that made Carlos my legal guardian so I had to move in with him. I got this little room with a ceiling fan. It ain't shit really, but it's better than one of them juvy hotels.

Carlos won't go to the hospital or nothin cuz besides

bein stubborn when the Steel Mill shut down they
stopped payin his health insurance. He worked for
them niggas for like fifteen years and they just gonna
up and drop him. They wouldn't even pay him no
pension.
  During the last week of school he started goin blind
and I had to stay at the crib and help him.

MOLLY: That's so sweet.

STROMILE: Changin that niggas' diapers ain't sweet,
Molly, trust me. Wakin up to some man you barely
know screamin in the middle of the night ain't sweet...
He wants me to kill him.

MOLLY: He does?

STROMILE: He wants me to put a pillow over his head
in the middle of the night. He wants me to do it this
weekend.

MOLLY: Are you gonna do it?

STROMILE: I don't know, Molly. He in a lotta pain....
That last week of school you prolly thought I was out
gang-bangin or some shit.

MOLLY: I didn't think that.

STROMILE: Yes you did. You thought I was one of those
South Lock niggas sellin crack at the bus station.

*(She kisses him again. The kiss lasts longer this time.
An awkward silence)*

MOLLY: Do you miss your mom?

STROMILE: Yeah, I miss that junky bitch.

(Pause)

MOLLY: So what do you wanna do with your life,
anyway?

STROMILE: I don't know. Nothin.

MOLLY: Come on.

STROMILE: Ain't shit to do. Grow old.

MOLLY: If you had your choice.

STROMILE: Choice.

MOLLY: If someone showed up with a million dollars.

STROMILE: I wouldn't want no million dollars. Money just makes you greedy.

MOLLY: Ten thousand, then.

STROMILE: I'd take ten gees.

MOLLY: What would you do with it?

STROMILE: I don't know. I always wanted to be a veterinarian.

MOLLY: Really?

STROMILE: On god.

MOLLY: You like animals?

STROMILE: They better than people.

MOLLY: You got pets or somethin?

STROMILE: We can't have no pets in that little-ass apartment.

MOLLY: Then how do you know you like em?

STROMILE: You ever been to the dog track?

MOLLY: Not yet. But I hear about it all the time. Ricky and Nolan bet on the races every day. Why?

STROMILE: Well, I worked there last summer. You know anything about greyhound racing?

MOLLY: A little.

STROMILE: Well, Gompers Park is the last track on the circuit. It's where they send all the slow dogs at the end

of the season. If you a slow dog and you come to
Gompers and win, then you might get to race again
next season. It's like a last chance and shit.

At the track I worked for this big white security guard
called Psycho Todd. When the races was done for the
day, all the dogs that didn't finish high got put in this
one kennel and it was my job to walk em one-by-one to
this loading dock on the other side of the track where
this old Italian nigga called Perotta would take em
away in a trailer. Every time I'd give him a dog he'd
give me some money. Sometimes I would make like
sixty bones and me and Psycho Todd would split it.

At the end of the summer I asked Psycho Todd what
Perotta was doin with them greyhounds and he told me
he was takin em to this farm and letting the dogs run so
he could hunt em with a machine gun. I thought he was
takin em to this adoption program in Quincy....

MOLLY: That's horrible.

STROMILE: Them dogs was sad, Molly. You could see it
in the way they walked. All slumped and tired. It was
like they knew what was comin.

MOLLY: Did you hear about what Shoe and Nolan
found?

STROMILE: All I know is it's somethin Dent keep in a
box and he won't show nobody.

MOLLY: It's a greyhound. A puppy.

STROMILE: For real?

MOLLY: For real. It's gold.

STROMILE: It's gold?

MOLLY: Gold.

STROMILE: Like gold gold?

MOLLY: Uh-huh. At first I thought it was fake. It's got
blue eyes, too.

STROMILE: Blue eyes!

MOLLY: Yep.

STROMILE: On a *dog*?

MOLLY: I'm not lyin.

STROMILE: That shit is bananas. Where'd they find it?

MOLLY: Under one of those new ficus trees on the waterfront. No one's sposed to know about it. They haven't even told Apache.

STROMILE: You saw it?

MOLLY: I looked in the box when Dent was in the bathroom. It was weird, Stromile. I couldn't stop starin at it. It made me so happy. I had this feeling that everything was gonna be okay.

STROMILE: For the baby?

MOLLY: Just everything.

(More fireworks explode. MOLLY *is startled. She reaches into her pocket, removes the pack of cigarettes, takes one, puts it in her mouth. He shoots her a look.)*

MOLLY: I'm just tastin it.

*(*STROMILE *takes the cigarette out of her mouth, throws it in the water. He stares at her stomach.)*

MOLLY: What?

*(*STROMILE *hesitates.)*

MOLLY: You wanna feel it again?

*(*STROMILE *nods.* MOLLY *takes his hand, places it under her shirt, on her stomach. The sound of ascending voices)*

*(*STROMILE *retracts his hand. He stands very quickly.)*

STROMILE: I better go.

MOLLY: When can I see you again?

STROMILE: I don't know. Soon. *(He turns to exit down the other end of the bridge.)*

MOLLY: Stromile.

(STROMILE stops, turns.)

MOLLY: Do you wish it was yours?

STROMILE: What.

MOLLY: The baby.

STROMILE: People comin, Molly. *(He turns, exits down the bridge.)*

(After a moment, MOLLY takes out her cigarettes, removes one, lights it, smokes. The fireworks continue to explode above her.)

Scene Three

(Saturday night. After the fireworks)

(The waterfront)

(A picnic table. A trash can. A newly planted ficus tree)

(The POLICEMAN is picking up forty ounce bottles of beer and setting them in the trash, humming a song.)

(WHITE STEVE enters holding the cardboard box from ACT ONE, Scene One. He sees the POLICEMAN, stops, tries to slowly back away.)

POLICEMAN: I see you there, little man.

(WHITE STEVE freezes. The POLICEMAN turns to him.)

POLICEMAN: Still doin business, huh?

WHITE STEVE: Not wif you.

POLICEMAN: You find a buyer for your sword?

WHITE STEVE: Maybe.

POLICEMAN: I'll bet you did.... You know, you lucky. They used to have a curfew here in Gompers. If you was under eighteen you couldn't be on the street past ten-thirty. What's your name again?

WHITE STEVE: Stromile.

POLICEMAN: Don't play games with me, son.

WHITE STEVE: It is. It's Stromile Cutler.

POLICEMAN: You Steve White. Everybody calls you White Steve.

WHITE STEVE: If you know my name then why'd you ask?

POLICEMAN: Just seein what you'd say. You realize I'm an officer of the law, don't you?

WHITE STEVE: So?

POLICEMAN: So you should trust me.

WHITE STEVE: I don't trust cops.

POLICEMAN: Why not?

WHITE STEVE: Cuz they just beat on you and take your money.

POLICEMAN: Some do, I'll admit it. But most are good. We civil servants, Steve. We on your side.... (He drops a few forty bottles in the trash.) All this alcohol. Mindless. Ignorant. You know what malt liquor is, Steve?

WHITE STEVE: Good.

POLICEMAN: It's the scum. And it's more potent cuz it's concentrated. Forty ounces of Old E ain't the same as forty ounces of Miller or Budweiser. The government pushes it into the ghettos and the poor areas cuz it promotes violence. One nigga kill another they got two less to worry about. One go in the ground and the other go to prison. You see, they think we a prime target now

cuz the Steel Mill closed and we down on our luck.
They think Gompers is one big ghetto. But they
mistaken, Steve. We got improvements just on the
horizon. The gambling boat. Little coffee shops.
New businesses springing up all along the riverfront.
All of it. They can push they malt liquor somewhere
else.... I'm tryin to hit you off with some knowledge,
Steve.

WHITE STEVE: I got knowledge.

POLICEMAN: Yeah? What kinda knowledge you got?

WHITE STEVE: I know stuff.

POLICEMAN: Yeah, you know how to jimmy a window.
You know how to boost you a pack of Newports at the
White Hen when the cashier got her back turned.

WHITE STEVE: Newports is nasty.

POLICEMAN: What school are you enrolled in for the
fall, Steve?

WHITE STEVE: What?

POLICEMAN: What school are you enrolled in?

WHITE STEVE: I ain't rolled in none of em.

POLICEMAN: Why not?

WHITE STEVE: I just moved here.

POLICEMAN: Well, you better get yourself registered.
You don't wanna be no truant do you? You in junior
high, right? Seventh, eighth grade?

WHITE STEVE: I'm older'n that!

POLICEMAN: You sure about that, Steve?

WHITE STEVE: I'm old, G!

POLICEMAN: Well you just make sure to get your old ass in school this fall. I don't wanna see you on the street, you hear?

WHITE STEVE: I ain't gonna be on the street.

POLICEMAN: What's in the box, anyway?

WHITE STEVE: Nothin.

POLICEMAN: Looks like a pretty heavy lookin nothin the way you strugglin.

WHITE STEVE: It ain't heavy.

POLICEMAN: You need me to help you?

WHITE STEVE: No.

(The POLICEMAN *starts toward* WHITE STEVE.*)*

WHITE STEVE: I said I don't need no help.

POLICEMAN: Your arms is shakin, Steve.

WHITE STEVE: Don't come no closer.

POLICEMAN: I'm tryin to help you, Steve.

WHITE STEVE: I'll stick you you come too close.

POLICEMAN: You'll stick me?

WHITE STEVE: Yup.

POLICEMAN: Why you gonna stick me?

WHITE STEVE: You'll see.

POLICEMAN: I will, huh? *(He takes another step.)*

POLICEMAN: You know it's against the law to threaten a policeman.

WHITE STEVE: It ain't a threat.

POLICEMAN: It ain't huh?

WHITE STEVE: Nope.

POLICEMAN: What is it, a promise?

WHITE STEVE: Somethin like that.

POLICEMAN: *(Continuing toward* WHITE STEVE*)* Whatchu gonna stick me with, Steve, huh? You got somethin for me, little man?

*(*WHITE STEVE *sets the box down, stands in front of it.)*

(The POLICEMAN *holds his hand out.)*

POLICEMAN: Lemme see what you got in that box, Steve. Come on now.

(From behind his back, WHITE STEVE *produces the hypodermic needle he showed* STROMILE *and* MOLLY *at the end of ACT ONE, Scene Two. He sticks the* POLICEMAN *on the back of his hand very quickly. The* POLICEMAN *grabs his hand.)*

WHITE STEVE: You gonna die, now, fuckin pig!

*(*WHITE STEVE *grabs his box and runs into the darkness.)*

(The POLICEMAN *reaches into his pocket and removes a white handkerchief. He presses it to the back of his hand, removes it. It is bloody.)*

Scene Four

(Saturday night)

(Apartment 4)

(The playing cards are scattered all over the floor. The bottle of vodka is half-empty. MRS GEORGE *is listening to music. Perhaps Bee Gees. She dances with the record album in her arms.)*

(A knock on the door. MRS GEORGE *dances to the door, opens it.* DENT *stands in the entrance. He is still well-dressed, perhaps a bit disheveled. He is holding a small arrangement of flowers.)*

DENT: How's it goin, Mrs George?

MRS GEORGE: The landlord!

DENT: Super.

MRS GEORGE: Superduper! Come to collect the rent?

DENT: You just paid the rent. I received a money order from your son two days ago.

MRS GEORGE: My music too loud?

DENT: I haven't had any complaints.

MRS GEORGE: Well, if you've come to evict us, it's gonna have to wait till tomorrow cause I'm havin too much fun.

(She dances in the doorway a bit. DENT watches her.)

MRS GEORGE: Who are the flowers for?

DENT: Molly.

MRS GEORGE: That's so sweet.

DENT: Yeah, you know.

MRS GEORGE: You're such a sweety.

DENT: Is Mol around?

MRS GEORGE: She went to the fireworks.

DENT: Did she say when she would be home?

MRS GEORGE: When they're finished. I thought she was with you.

DENT: We had a bit of a disagreement.

MRS GEORGE: Oh no. I'm sorry.

DENT: It's no big deal. We'll sort it out.

MRS GEORGE: Wanna come in?

DENT: I don't know, Mrs George. I'm sorta in a bind.

MRS GEORGE: Oh, everyone's in a bind these days, Richard. Come in and play for a minute.

(DENT *enters. She closes the door behind him, takes his hand, they dance a bit.)*

MRS GEORGE: Not bad for a landlord.

DENT: Super.

MRS GEORGE: Superduperpooperscooper.

(They dance a bit more, then she almost falls. He catches her. They knock the record player. The record stops. She laughs.)

DENT: Whoa, horsy.

MRS GEORGE: Horsy's thirsty. Horsy wantsa drink. Wanna drink? I got vodka and vodka.

DENT: I'll have vodka.

MRS GEORGE: Tonic?

DENT: Sure.

MRS GEORGE: *(Referring to the flowers)* I'll put those in some water.

(She takes the flowers from him, exits to the kitchen.)

DENT: Mrs George, you haven't seen a box floatin around, have you?

MRS GEORGE: A who?

DENT: A box. A plain cardboard box. About yay-big. It's missin from my apartment. I had some important papers in it.

MRS GEORGE: A floating box with important papers. Sounds mysterious. *(Entering with drinks)* Richard Dent, International Man of Mystery. *(She hands him his drink.)* Cheers.

DENT: Cheers.

(They clink glasses, drink.)

MRS GEORGE: To Molly.

DENT: To Molly.

(They clink glasses, drink.)

MRS GEORGE: And the baby.

DENT: To Molly and the baby.

(They clink glasses, drink again.)

MRS GEORGE: And to keepin it in the family.

DENT: And to keepin it in the family.

(They clink glasses, drink again.)

MRS GEORGE: And to all the king's horses and all the king's men.

DENT: That too.

(They clink glasses, drink again.)

MRS GEORGE: To toasts that never end.

DENT: To toasts that never end.

(They clink glasses, drink again.)

MRS GEORGE: To never ending toasts.

DENT: To never ending toasts.

(They clink glasses, drink again.)

MRS GEORGE: You're fun.

DENT: I'm glad someone thinks so.

MRS GEORGE: Molly must have a good time with you.

(Awkward pause)

DENT: Mrs George, would you mind if—

MRS GEORGE: Call me Pam, Richard. Please.

DENT: Pam.

MRS GEORGE: You know, I'm not that much older than you. When did you graduate high school, anyway?

DENT: Eighty-five.

MRS GEORGE: I was Eighty.

DENT: Really?

MRS GEORGE: Don't be so surprised! We were practically classmates. Go Steelmen!

DENT: Go Steelmen!

MRS GEORGE: Shishboombah!

DENT: Shishboombah!

(They clink glasses, drink. MRS GEORGE drains hers.)

MRS GEORGE: I'm gonna have another one. You don't mind, do you?

DENT: Knock yourself out.

(She exits to the kitchen again.)

MRS GEORGE: Hey, you were a basketball player, right?

DENT: I was.

MRS GEORGE: Yeah, I remember you. After I came back from nurses' training I went to a game with one of my girlfriends. You were a real hotshot.

DENT: I had my moments.

MRS GEORGE: Did you play in college?

DENT: I didn't even go. I blew my knee out the summer after I graduated. Lost my scholarship.

MRS GEORGE: Well, that's too bad.

DENT: Kay sirah, sirah, you know?

MRS GEORGE: I think college is a good thing.

DENT: *(Checking his watch)* It is what it is.

MRS GEORGE: Mol wants to go to G C C and study Business Administration... I wish I woulda stayed in nurses' training, I'll tell you that much... Woulda, coulda, shoulda, you know? *(She returns with a fresh drink.)*

MRS GEORGE: Richard Dent.

DENT: Pam George.

MRS GEORGE: Here's to hotshots.

DENT: To hotshots.

(They clink glasses, drink. She touches his face, almost absentmindedly, then retracts her hand. An awkward pause)

DENT: Pam, Would you mind if I checked Molly's room?

MRS GEORGE: Check it for what?

DENT: That cardboard box I was telling you about.

MRS GEORGE: Not at all. But don't be long, you'll miss the party.

DENT: I'll be quick, I promise. *(He sets is drink down, exits to MOLLY's room.)*

(While he is gone, MRS GEORGE checks her breath, smells her pits, fixes her hair in the reflection of the T V. DENT returns.)

MRS GEORGE: Is it in there?

DENT: I'm afraid not.

MRS GEORGE: Well, if I see any floating boxes I'll be sure to knock on your door.

DENT: I'd appreciate that.

(Pause)

MRS GEORGE: So you think you're ready to be a father, Richard Dent?

DENT: I don't know. I haven't really thought about it much.

MRS GEORGE: Cocky.

DENT: No, I just figure instinct will take over. Like the apes, you know?

MRS GEORGE: It takes a helluva lot more than instinct, I can promise you that. The screamin and cryin. Dirty diapers. Five a.m. feedings. But it's worth it. It'll change your life forever, that's for sure.

DENT: That's what I hear.

MRS GEORGE: Hey, stay right there. I gotta show you somethin.

(She exits to the kitchen. DENT *checks his watch again. Moments later,* MRS GEORGE *returns with* WHITE STEVE's *sword.)*

MRS GEORGE: *(Killing an invisible foe)* Hyaah!!

*(*DENT *almost jumps out of his skin.* MRS GEORGE *laughs.)*

DENT: Jesus, Mrs George!

(She points the sword at him.)

DENT: I mean Pam!

MRS GEORGE: *(Lowering the sword, turning it in her hand)* Pretty neat, huh?

DENT: Where'd you get that thing?

MRS GEORGE: Some little kid sold it to me. Knocked on my door this afternoon. I bought it for ten bucks. As he described it, it's an authentic kilitary mutlass. I mean military cutlass! He was so cute I couldn't resist.

(She hands the sword to him. He studies it for a moment.)

DENT: Looks like the real deal to me. *(He hands it back to her.)* I better get goin, Pam. Tell Mol I came by. Thanks for the drink.

(MRS GEORGE *points the sword at him, playful but threatening.*)

MRS GEORGE: Be still, soldier!

DENT: Be still?

MRS GEORGE: Yeah, stand down! Be still! Hold your position! Colonel Pam wantsa get to know you better.

(DENT *puts his hands up playfully, sits on the sofa.*)

MRS GEORGE: Whattaya thinka me, anyway?

DENT: What do I think of you?

MRS GEORGE: Yeah.

DENT: In terms of what?

MRS GEORGE: In terms of do you think I'm an attractive woman?

DENT: Like sexually attractive?

MRS GEORGE: No, automotively attractive. Of course, sexually attractive!

DENT: Well, it's a funny thing to be askin your daughter's boyfriend.

MRS GEORGE: We're all adults here, Richard. Come on, humor me.

DENT: Sure, I think you're attractive.

MRS GEORGE: How do I compare to Molly?

DENT: Now that's not fair.

MRS GEORGE: Answer the question.

DENT: You're sorta puttin me on the spot, Pam.

MRS GEORGE: Oh, spot, shmot. I wanna know. And be honest. I can handle it.

DENT: I think you're both very pretty.

MRS GEORGE: She's gotta better ass, though, right?

DENT: Pam...

MRS GEORGE: No, I admit it.

DENT: Your daughter's got a very well-proportioned ass, yes. But you look great, too.

MRS GEORGE: When you hit forty, things just start saggin, you know? I had a great ass in my day, Richard.

DENT: I'm sure you did, Pam.

MRS GEORGE: I still have a great ass. Just not as great as Molly's... I'll let you in on a little secret.

DENT: Okay.

MRS GEORGE: I used to dance for a living.

DENT: You were a stripper?

MRS GEORGE: Just for a little while. After Molly's father took off and before I got my job at the mill we were pretty desperate. Food stamps and government cheese, you know?

DENT: Sure.

MRS GEORGE: I was pretty good at it. I made six hundred dollars one night.

DENT: I'm impressed.

(MRS GEORGE *starts to dance rather suggestively with the saber. It's somewhat slow and playful but then evolves into something a little dangerous. She either sings or hums along, perhaps some old Prince.* DENT *plays the role of the client, clapping, catcalling, taking money out of his wallet, etc. She takes his drink out of his hand, downs it, spills a bit down her front, laughs.*)

MRS GEORGE: Not so bad, right?

DENT: Who woulda thought?

(She reaches down, feels his crotch.)

DENT: Whoa, tiger.

MRS GEORGE: Mmmmm. I bet you got a nice one.
Do you got a nice one, Richard?

DENT: Um, Mrs George—I mean Pam—

MRS GEORGE: I wanna put you in my mouth, Richard.
Whattaya say, huh?

DENT: I don't think that's such a good idea.

(He stands. She stands, puts the saber under his chin.)

MRS GEORGE: I think it's a great idea. I think it's the best
idea I've had in a long time.

*(With her free hand, she feels his crotch some more. She kisses
him wetly on the mouth. They make out for a moment and
then she drops the saber, kneels down in front of him, starts
to take his pants down.)*

DENT: Um, Pam...

(She has taken him in her mouth, now.)

DENT: Whoa... Maybe we should—Jesus that's
good—like go in the other room or somethin...
Oh, Jesus that's so good...

*(Just before DENT comes, the front door opens, closes.
MOLLY enters the living room)*

DENT: Mol.

*(MRS GEORGE stands very quickly, covers her mouth.
MOLLY watches them for a moment, then turns and quickly
exits. DENT fixes his pants, stands, grabs the flowers, exits.)*

Scene Five

(Early Sunday morning. Well before sunrise)

(The train bridge)

*(NOLAN is sitting in the middle of the train bridge, holding
FINN's noose that he obtained from ACT TWO, Scene One.
He undoes his shirt, to reveal heavy bandages. They are
bloodstained. He touches the bandages, closes his shirt.
Moments later, SHOE appears. He is in drag, wearing a long
dress. He carries a purse and walks in heels. He is also
wearing a wig and his face is made up like a woman's.)*

SHOE: Hey.

NOLAN: Hey.

SHOE: Great stars, huh?

NOLAN: Uh-huh.

SHOE: I've never seen so many. Anybody else up here?

NOLAN: Nuh-uh.

SHOE: You sure?

NOLAN: I'm the only one.

SHOE: What's that you're holding?

NOLAN: A rope.

SHOE: There's a noose on the end of it.

NOLAN: This is the way I found it.

SHOE: What are you planning on doing with it?

NOLAN: I'm just carryin around.

SHOE: Oh. Okay.

(Pause)

NOLAN: Did Dent find the box yet?

SHOE: Not yet. He's sorta freaking out. He was with Dragan when I left. Apparently Apache knows about it.

NOLAN: That was inevitable.

SHOE: Yeah, I think shit's gonna hit the fan if it doesn't turn up.

NOLAN: It'll turn up.

(SHOE *walks over to* NOLAN. NOLAN *stands.*)

SHOE: Hi.

NOLAN: Hi.

SHOE: I missed you... Did you miss me?

NOLAN: Sure.

SHOE: Do I look nice?

NOLAN: Yeah, you look good.

SHOE: It took me like an hour to get ready. You like the heels?

NOLAN: Uh-huh.

SHOE: Last time you didn't like my shoes so I got these. I ordered them from this catalog. Size thirteen. They were a hundred and thirty bucks. *(He showcases the shoes a bit.)* So can I have a hug?

(SHOE *steps closer to* NOLAN. *They hug.*)

SHOE: You feel good.

NOLAN: I do?

SHOE: Yeah. Do you like the way I feel?

NOLAN: Uh-huh.

SHOE: Kiss me.

(They kiss. It gets a little intense. NOLAN *pulls away.)*

SHOE: What?

NOLAN: Nothin.

SHOE: Do I have bad breath or somethin?

NOLAN: No.

SHOE: You weren't using your tongue.

NOLAN: So?

SHOE: You always use your tongue, Nolan. Is my face rough? I shaved twice the way you like it.

NOLAN: Your face is fine.

SHOE: What is it then?

NOLAN: I thought I heard someone.

(They listen.)

SHOE: It's just the wind.

(SHOE tries to take NOLAN's hand. NOLAN pulls away)

SHOE: What's wrong?

NOLAN: I don't know, Shoe.

SHOE: Julius.

NOLAN: Julius.

SHOE: You don't know what?

NOLAN: ...Fuck.

SHOE: Just tell me. Please.

NOLAN: I can't handle this.

SHOE: This meaning what?

NOLAN: Being a fag.

SHOE: Please don't use that word.

NOLAN: Sorry... Being gay. I can't.... I mean, I grew up thinking....

SHOE: You told me you always knew.

NOLAN: I did. But that doesn't matter. I mean the guys at the mill....

SHOE: They shut the mill down, Nolan.

NOLAN: I know, but....

SHOE: There are no more guys at the mill.

(Pause)

NOLAN: What's it gonna be like when we get old?

SHOE: I don't know, Nolan. But hopefully we'll be together.

NOLAN: Always hiding it. All that shame.

SHOE: We don't have to hide it. And it doesn't have to be shameful.

NOLAN: Shoe, when was the last time you saw two queers walkin around Gompers?

SHOE: We could go somewhere where we wouldn't have to hide it.

NOLAN: Where?

SHOE: There are cities. San Francisco. Chicago. There's this place in New York City called Chelsea. We could go there.... I'd leave tomorrow if I knew you'd go with me. I'd drop everything.

NOLAN: Don't waste your time with me, okay?

SHOE: I love you, Nolan. You're the only person I've ever loved. And I know you love me too.

NOLAN: You're wrong.

SHOE: You've said it out loud.

NOLAN: I was lying.

SHOE: Don't deny this, Nolan. Please...

(SHOE *takes a step toward* NOLAN. NOLAN *takes a step
back.* SHOE *reaches for* NOLAN'*s hand.* NOLAN *pulls away.*
SHOE *reaches again.* NOLAN *pulls away.)*

SHOE: Why are you doing this?

NOLAN: Don't touch me, Shoe.

SHOE: Julius!

NOLAN: It's over, Julius, okay?

SHOE: No.

(SHOE *grabs* NOLAN'*s arm. They grapple a bit, and then*
NOLAN *slips the noose over* SHOE'*s head, cinches it tight,
he strangles him for a moment, pulls* SHOE *to the ground.)*

NOLAN: It's over, okay?! It's fucking over!!

(NOLAN *kicks* SHOE *in the stomach.* SHOE *collapses, gasping
for air.* NOLAN *hovers for a moment and then exits down the
other side of the bridge holding his stomach.)*

(*Moments later,* WHITE STEVE *appears from the other side of
the train bridge holding the box. He approaches* SHOE *very
slowly.)*

WHITE STEVE: Hey, Lady.

(SHOE *turns, looks at* WHITE STEVE *for a moment, turns
back.)*

WHITE STEVE: Hey, lady, you okay?

(SHOE *slowly rises, loosens the noose around his neck,
keeping his back to* WHITE STEVE.)

WHITE STEVE: Lady, you ain't seen ten bucks up here
have you? I lost it earlier. I had it in my pocket. I don't
know where that shit went. You seen it?

(SHOE *shakes his head.)*

WHITE STEVE: You know there's this man out there on the water. He's like fishin or some shit. I seen him earlier. He's blue.... Canya talk, lady?

(No response)

WHITE STEVE: Hey, lady, check out what I got. *(He moves closer.)* I bet you ain't never seen nothin like this before. I'm sellin it. I'd let you have it for twenty bucks. Look, lady.

(SHOE turns around. WHITE STEVE stares at him for a moment, then takes a step back.)

WHITE STEVE: Shoe? ...Is that you Shoe? ...Aw, snap.

(WHITE STEVE starts for the other end of the bridge, drops the box, picks it up, descends with the box. After a moment, SHOE sits in the middle of the bridge, cries.)

Scene Six

(Early Sunday morning. Just before dawn)

(Apartment 5, the courtyard apartment, apartment 4, the waterfront.)

(In Apartment 5, CARLOS is sitting up in bed. He is wearing a pair of red pajamas. There is a single light on. He is holding his cassette recorder. He presses play and the sound of a trombone issues forth. It is a different arrangement from the one at the end of ACT ONE. The trombone plays for a moment and then CARLOS sings the following song over the course of the rest of the scene.)

CARLOS: *(Singing)* Billy's baby doll hands
Grandpa's grandfather clock
The river's turning to chocolate
I'll love you down by the dock

Peter's pastry of peppers
Henry's hat full of hay

His eyes were blackberries
Don't let the inquest dismay

Little Sadman where did you go?
I'm afraid I've been lost in the snow
Little Sadman it's lonely at night
I forgot how to turn out the light

(At the waterfront, the POLICEMAN *walks by. His hand is
bandaged. He seems somehow lost. From the picnic table,
he removes an empty forty-ounce beer bottle, looks at it for
a moment, then sets it back on the picnic table and
continues walking.)*

(After he has exited, MOLLY *appears. She is
hyperventilating, walking with great difficulty.
She lurches toward the picnic table, sits for a moment,
pulls out the hammer and a glass bottle half-filled with
a blue liquid. She sets both items it in front of her,
buries her face in her hands.)*

CARLOS: *(Singing)* The stars are like oysters
The sky is the sea
I think I'll go fishing
In the old willow tree

The birds rule the lions
A fish caught a bear
Mother Nature's been dreaming
There's a storm in her hair

*(*MOLLY *rises, moves away from the picnic table, crosses to
the ficus tree. She reaches down. From behind the tree she
removes the cardboard box. She stares into it, smiles, reaches
inside, removes a golden greyhound puppy. It is dead.
She takes it in her arms, slides down the trunk of the tree,
sits staring out at the water. After a moment, she rises,
crosses back to the picnic table, stares at the hammer and
the glass bottle of blue liquid.)*

CARLOS: *(Singing)* Little Sadman where did you go?
I'm afraid I've been lost in the snow
Little Sadman it's lonely at night
I forgot how to turn out the light

*(In Apartment 4, MRS GEORGE is seated on the floor.
Her hair is disheveled and the T V is on. She regards the
empty bottle of vodka for a moment, looks around, then
begins to gather the scattered playing cards. When she has
them all in hand, she slowly deals herself a game of solitaire.)*

*(In Apartment 2, DENT is sitting at the kitchen table, holding
the flowers that were intended for MOLLY.)*

CARLOS: *(Singing)* I found a bowlegged rooster
And a cat with three tails
There's a pigeon-toed monkey
Eating peanuts and snails

At the circus I saw him
Redirecting his frown
The Big-top exploded
The tigers bullwhipped the clowns

*(In the courtyard apartment, the kitchen window is opened
and WHITE STEVE climbs through. He is winded, afraid.
The lights in the kitchen are out except for one, perhaps over
the stove. Over the back of one of the chairs, FINN has draped
his dress greens.)*

*(WHITE STEVE crosses to the refrigerator, opens it quietly,
removes a plate of ham. He eats several slices, puts the plate
back in the refrigerator, shuts the door. He then crosses to the
table, where he spots the three coffee cups form ACT TWO,
Scene One. He looks into each cup and then grabs FINN's.
He drinks from it, guzzling the whole thing, then sets it
down. He burps. After a moment, he spots FINN's dress
greens. He giggles a bit, then puts on the jacket and the
pants over his clothes. He pulls the trombone case out from
under the table, opens it, removes the trombone, and begins*

marching around the kitchen table, pretending to play the
trombone. After one or two circles, he collapses.)

CARLOS: *(Singing)* And the clouds cry a hailstorm
And the oceans catch fire
When the whales fly to heaven
Will the North Star expire?

(In the Courtyard Apartment, FINN enters the kitchen.
He is wearing boxer shorts, a stained T-shirt, black socks,
an old housecoat. He sees WHITE STEVE collapsed on
the floor in his dress greens, his trombone next to him.
He crosses to WHITE STEVE, goes to his knees, feels his pulse,
pulls himself up on a chair, sits very still, then pulls the
American flag off the table, bends down, and begins to roll
WHITE STEVE in the flag.)

CARLOS: *(Singing)* Little Sadman where did you go?
I'm afraid I've been lost in the snow
Little Sadman it's lonely at night
I forgot how to turn out the light
Please help me turn out the light

(In Apartment 5, STROMILE appears beside CARLOS' bed.
He is holding a pillow. STROMILE puts his hand on CARLOS'
shoulder. CARLOS smiles. STROMILE turns out the light.)

Scene Seven

(The waterfront)

(Sunday morning. Dawn)

(MOLLY is under the ficus tree, the box next to her. She is
holding the hammer. The glass bottle is still on the picnic
table, empty.)

(The sound of someone walking out of the water toward the
shore. Moments later, SHOE appears. He is drenched and still
wearing the dress. His wig is gone, though, as are his shoes

*and purse. The makeup is grotesquely smeared on his face.
The noose is still hanging around his neck. It appears to have
snapped a few feet from the knot point.)*

(He crosses to MOLLY, *regards her for a moment. They share
a look. After a moment,* SHOE *reaches down, and takes the
box. He stares into it. His face doesn't change. He exits with
the box.)*

*(*STROMILE *enters with his book bag. He approaches* MOLLY
*slowly. She stands. They face each other for a moment.
He offers his hand.)*

(Lights fade on the waterfront.)

END OF PLAY

www.ingramcontent.com/pod-product-compliance
Lightning Source LLC
Chambersburg PA
CBHW052130090426
42741CB00009B/2031